The Chattanooga Lookouts
& 100 Seasons of Scenic City Baseball

Stephen Martini

Published by
Dry Ice Publishing
Cleveland, TN 37323
Visit our Web site at www.lulu.com/dryicepublishing

Printed by
Lulu Enterprises
3131 RDU Center Drive, Suite 210
Morrisville, NC 27560

Cover Photography and Layout
J. Guy Photography
Chattanooga, Tennessee
www.jguyphoto.com

"On the Cover" – (Front) Chattanooga Lookouts Infielder Gary Patchett
takes a cut at a pitch in a game against the Carolina Mudcats August 4th,
2005. (Back) The scoreboard at BellSouth Park records a tied score of the
same game in the bottom of the ninth, as the Lookouts face two outs and
a full-count. The Lookouts won the game 7 to 6.

International Standard Book Number (ISBN): 978-0-557-27927-2
Printed in the United States of America

First Paperback Printing: April 2006

This book is dedicated to Hillis Layne –
A legendary piece in the puzzle of the national pastime and
Chattanooga's most famous unsung hero.

Acknowledgments

Writing a book like this – trying to piece together the events of the past 125 years and 100 seasons of Chattanooga baseball – is a huge undertaking that is summed up best by author Leo Rosten, who said, "The only reason for being a professional writer is that you can't help it."

I owe a debt of thanks to many people, likely more than I'll remember to list. But here's my shot at it:

First and foremost, God. He sees all; He knows all; and without Him I'm as effective as a sack of leaves on the curb in November.

Thank you to my wife, Tina, and son, Zachary, for loving a writer and spending your days, nights, weekends, and holidays reading about, talking about, and hearing about the Chattanooga Lookouts. I promise I'm done talking about my books … until the next one.

Thanks to my dad and mom, Tony and Tonya Martini, for encouraging a geeky first-grader to read and write … then making me go outside and play ball with my brother like a normal kid when all I wanted to do was shut myself in my room with my nose in a book.

Thanks, Hillis Layne and Roy Hawes, two true gems in Lookouts history, for their willingness to share their stories with me and their winning attitudes and abilities with Chattanooga.

Thanks, Frank Burke, for continuing to share the vision of Chattanooga Lookouts baseball – and mine.

Thanks, Jonathan Guy, for dominating the camera lens and producing such high quality photos for my words to rest between.

Thanks, Charlie Timmons, for giving 25 years as a firefighter with the city of Chattanooga protecting her citizens and 27 years to the fans of Lookouts baseball entertaining their ears.

Thanks, Bill Hull, curator at the Chattanooga Regional History Museum, and their crackerjack staff who work daily to preserve the heritage of the Scenic City.

Thanks to the staff at the Chattanooga Hamilton County Bicenntenial Library's Local History Department for their knowledgeable assistance.

Thanks, Gary and Becky Adams, my in-laws, and Mitch Smith for production assistance.

Thanks, Kim Kinsey, Joyce Richey, Jason Jones (for purchasing the first copy) and the entire third shift crew at the Chattanooga Police Department's dispatch center for technical assistance and pointers.

Thanks, Bill Lee, Arvin Reingold, Harmon Jolley, Woodrow W. Benefield, and Dan Creed for filling in the holes.

Thanks, Wirt Gammon, Jr., for pointing me in the right direction.

Thanks to the entire staff at BellSouth Park for being helpful each and every time I wandered through the door to the front office for yet another interview, or throughout the stadium in pursuit of the perfect picture. Further, I am eternally grateful and humbled you cleared some space on a shelf in your gift shop for my labor of love and consuming passion – this little book.

"Whoever wants to know the heart and mind of America had better learn baseball."

- Jacques Barzun, historian

CONTENTS

Preface

You won't find the story of a minor league baseball team in statistics. The win-loss columns of the newspaper don't tell the tales of legendary days at the park or outstanding promotions.

Rather, the story of minor league baseball lies within the fans that continue to support teams whose rosters change sometimes week-to-week.

It lies within the players, striving for years in the Bush Leagues for just one crack of the bat in the majors.

It lies within the hopes of every team owner, struggling to win the ongoing battle for America's rapidly diminishing attention span. Competing against cable television, air conditioning, and days at the lake for but a few hours of time spent lavishing in the presence of our national pastime.

The story is in the hearts of every eight-year-old boy holding a hot dog, a Coke, a large foam finger, and a baseball cap donning the logo of the hometown team. In almost every city, the story is the same. The same game adored by the same type of people on the same sunny summer days that make you wish, in that fleeting moment, you were a child again.

I've watched the story unfold all my life. Sitting by my Dad, baseball glove in my hand eagerly watching the field for any chance at catching a fly ball while cheering the Triple-A Tacoma Tigers and Salt Lake City Buzz, and the Pioneer League Ogden Raptors. When I grew up and got married, I introduced my wife to the game as we rooted for the Single A Kinston Indians.

But the greatest story of the greatest game lies in the heart of Chattanooga, wound tightly within the fabric of one of the oldest baseball leagues in the nation.

Today, I take my own son to cheer the Lookouts at BellSouth Park. I cheer them today for where they're going. I cheer them for where they've been because I know the story.

The story of one of the greatest baseball promoters in the history of the game.

The story of nine members of the National Baseball Hall of Fame.

The story of devoted fans, stunning upsets, saving graces, and unimaginable heartbreaks.

The story of empty stands and record crowds, golden ages and dark clouds, bench-clearing brawls and wedding bells, die-hard fans and championship seasons, and legendary players, both bragged on and banned.

I'll tell you the story of the Chattanooga Lookouts – arguably one of the most significant ball clubs in the history of this nation – the way the Lookouts have always told their story. Not through statistics, wins and losses, batting or earned run averages. Rather through their stories of one hundred seasons spent entertaining generations of fans in the same way they'll continue to entertain in the Scenic City of the South for generations to come.

Grab a Coke and a hot dog, or some Crackerjacks. Find a seat down one of the baselines, just out of the sun and settle in; the game is about to begin.

Chapter One

In the Beginning ...

Chattanooga.

The Scenic City of the South.

The South's little big town straddling the Tennessee-Georgia state line has been home to tourism since the turn of the 20th century.

At the top of Lookout Mountain, hundreds of thousands have flocked to "See Rock City" – for decades, a phrase emblazoned on the roofs of barns across the Southeast and Midwest. From Missionary Ridge to Point Park, the city is steeped in military history, telling the struggles of a nation divided in the midst of the Civil War.

Year-round, tourists come to Chattanooga to ride the Incline Railway and tour the Tennessee Aquarium – the world's largest freshwater aquatic exhibit.

The Scenic City of the South is the self-proclaimed home of miniature "putt-putt" golf – originally called "gooney golf". In the 1940s, Glenn Miller immortalized the Chattanooga Choo Choo in a chart-topping song.

Tourists flow into Chattanooga as strong and wide as the winding Tennessee River. Within the currents of that timeless river has always been baseball.

Almost since the birth of the game as a professional sport, Chattanooga has been home to organized baseball.

As Chattanooga struggled to acclimate to the turbulent aftermath of the Civil War – seeing the rise of the Ku Klux Klan and Jim Crow laws – a nation turned its battered eyes on baseball.

In 1869, Cincinnati, Ohio formed the first professional baseball team – the Red Stockings. In 1871, other cities fielded teams and joined with Cincinnati to form the first professional baseball league – the National Association.

By the end of the decade, semi-professional baseball swept downstream from Cincinnati and washed up on the shores of the Tennessee River along the banks of the Lookout Valley.

The seeds of the national pastime took root and semi-professional baseball budded in Chattanooga.

Baseball found a home with the Roane Iron Company in 1880, when the mill fielded an unbeatable team of employees called the Chattanooga Roanes. The Roanes were virtually unstoppable, routinely defeating the Mobile Pastimes, and teams in Nashville and Knoxville. When at home, the Roanes played on a ball field found at the corner of Douglas and Vine streets, now in the heart of the University of Tennessee at Chattanooga campus, near MacLellan Gym.

"Billy Hart"
One of only two Lookouts pitchers in 1885, Hart started his career in Chattanooga. After that season, he played for the Philadelphia Athletics, then Cincinnati and Brooklyn. In 1910, he was playing with the minor league club in Little Rock when O.B. Andrews bought the franchise and moved the club back to Chattanooga. At the end of the 1910 season, Hart retired – ending his career with the same club with which he'd started 25 years earlier.

Many big league teams from further north used the field for spring training games.

For five years, the Roanes dominated semi-professional baseball, priming the pump for fans of Chattanooga baseball to support a professional ball club.

In 1885, Chattanoogans got that chance.

Atlanta, Nashville, Birmingham, and Memphis united to form a professional baseball league. Chattanooga eagerly jumped in – along with Augusta, Macon, and Columbus forming the Southern League. The league is now one of the oldest in the history of the game.

Henry W. Grady, managing editor of the Atlanta Constitution, was league president. Spearheading Chattanooga's jump into professional baseball was a local banker and entrepreneur, John C. Stanton. In 1870, Stanton built a five-story extravagant hotel along what is now the 1400 block of Market Street. Construction costs mounted above $100,000 as did the amenities – indoor plumbing on every floor, billiard rooms, a barbershop, several balconies, a large dining room and a livery stable.

The Stanton House

The Stanton House was a risky venture, built well east of the city's growing downtown in an attempt to draw tourists to settle the area. Some feared Stanton's decision to build so far from Chattanooga would deter guests from staying at the hotel.

By 1885, after fifteen years in East Chattanooga, Stanton likely shared those fears.

Surely, he saw the rising popularity of baseball and watched as Chattanoogans embraced the Roanes.

This was the answer he sought! Baseball could bring fans to the Stanton House – fans he could convert into patrons of his hotel!

The banker built a baseball field behind his hotel, calling it Stanton Field. Players, barely paid but eager to play, came out to practice leaving behind their families and their other jobs for a few hours each day to chase a dream.

When the men took the field that spring, they faced a mountain of expectations. The Roanes were incredibly successful and the success of Stanton's club relied on their ability to win games.

In their inaugural season, Chattanooga won just 30 of 89 games. The club blamed their losses on a variety of things – lousy umpiring, un-sportsmanlike conduct by opposing team's fans, and some of their own players not performing to their potential.

Other teams wooed the Chattanooga ballplayers – Bentel, Ryan, and Seigle – with big salaries to throw the games.

"The players have been notified they will be blacklisted if they do not play better," a reporter for the Chattanooga Times wrote. "They will doubtless heed that warning."

Later, Bentel was suspended for being the ringleader of the scandal.

The Atlanta Crackers won the first Southern League pennant, while Chattanooga finished seventh of the eight teams – defeating only Birmingham.

Crowds came to Stanton Field but didn't stay, which was the story all across the newly formed Southern League. By the end of the 1885 season, Columbus disbanded their club.

In July 1886, Chattanooga dropped out of the league, unable to keep players away from their families and jobs for months at a time. When the club dropped out, they'd fallen to the bottom of the Southern League, winning just twenty of fifty-four games.

The Atlanta Crackers claimed the league pennant for the second time.

In 1887 and 1888, Chattanooga didn't rejoin the Southern League, unable to field a team. Still others – Mobile, Nashville, Atlanta, and Savannah – dropped out as well. In 1888, Chattanooga fielded a local semi-professional team called the Sullivans, but to no avail.

Refusing to quit, Stanton and the Chattanooga ballplayers rejoined the Southern League in 1889.

New Orleans, Atlanta, and Mobile jumped back into the league with Chattanooga, playing in front of budding fans for only a few months until the league suspended play in June to reorganize. After a three-week lapse in play, the teams returned to the diamond ready to resume the season.

Calamity continued and the Southern League folded for a second time that season – little more than two weeks later on July 5th. Atlanta, Birmingham, and Memphis struggled to draw fans, dropping out of the league before July. Chattanooga played only thirty-eight games that season, winning just over half to finish third. New Orleans claimed the pennant.

"Samuel Strang Nicklin" Not only was Nicklin a former player and owner of the Chattanooga Lookouts, he also coached baseball at West Point Military Academy. Under his tutelage – Five-star General Omar Nelson Bradley and General Robert Neyland, the now famous head coach of University of Tennessee football and namesake of the team's 104,079-capacity stadium on the banks of the Tennessee River.

For two years, the Southern League saw no action, players and fans opting to stay home and devote their time, money, and energy into their jobs and family. The game of baseball was simply that – a game – and these men couldn't afford to dedicate much of their sparse free time to play.

Regardless of what seemed to be a mountain of mounting obstacles, baseball promoters and owners pressed forward and, in 1892, the Southern League saw its third resurrection in eight years.

John Stanton let a contract to a Mr. Brown to build a better ball field for Chattanooga behind his hotel on what was then called Montgomery Avenue.

Chattanooga chose a team name – the Chatts – and manager, Ted Sullivan (no doubt the namesake of the city's semi-pro 1888 club) rallied his troops to do battle.

In the first half of the season, the Chatts dominated, besting Montgomery, Mobile, New Orleans, Atlanta, Macon, and Memphis. The Chatts won 52 of the 82 games they played and finished on top of the Southern League.

According to an article in the Chattanooga News, the crowds responded.

After a late-April victory put the Chatts back in control of the league pennant race, one reporter wrote, "The crowd was tremendous. [The crowd of 3,500] seemed nearly twice as many as the opening game of the league … the edges of the left and right field were covered with vehicles. The roofs of the ticket and refreshment stands were covered with spectators."

At one point, the games drew such large crowds many climbed on top of nearby railroad cars to catch a free peek at the action and avoiding the dime admission charge to sit by the field.

Strong crowd attendance through July wasn't enough to keep the Chatts winning. In the second half, they fell to last place in the league while Birmingham quickly stepped up, winning 30 of 41 games.

At the time, a champion was determined in a playoff series between the best team from the first and second halves. By season's end, Birmingham and Chattanooga set to face off in a best-of-nine series.

Both clubs immediately called in new players for the championship game, eager to claim the title. The move was nothing new for the Chattanooga club, according to author Wirt Gammon. In his book, Your Lookouts Since 1885 he wrote, "The personnel of the 'Nooga club was constantly changing anyhow, because the players and their fiery skipper couldn't get along for more than a change of the moon."

The first three games were fought in Birmingham, while the next three raged in Chattanooga. Game seven was played in Atlanta while Nashville hosted the final two games.

By the ninth game, each team claimed four wins and both teams played hard for the pennant in font of a huge crowd of Nashvillians. When the umpires called the ninth game on account of darkness and both teams were still scoreless, the officials decided the final game would be played out the next day.

The deciding battle never took place.

During the night, Birmingham "departed its several ways, the members restless to be home after five months of absence, scattering to the north, south, east and west."

When Ted Sullivan woke up the next morning to the news that his opponent fled the battlefield under cover of darkness, he was outraged.

The officials awarded the Chatts their first Southern League pennant title by default but Sullivan was not satisfied. The fiery manager wasn't content to win the title without winning a deciding game. He accused Birmingham of robbing Chattanooga of a legitimate pennant. Birmingham manager Mr. Manning replied only that his boys had business at home.

Chattanooga's official claim to the contested title lasted only a few months. At an October 31st meeting of the Southern League, officials awarded the Southern League pennant to Birmingham, citing the club posted better numbers throughout the season than Chattanooga.

Chattanooga still recognizes the 1892 pennant as its first Southern League Championship victory.

<u>Chapter Two</u>

"Tottering on the Raw Edge of Oblivion"

Despite claiming their first pennant-winning season, averaging around 800 fans at the field per game, Chattanooga struggled with the rest of the nation to keep interest in the sport.

Wrote one Chattanooga Times reporter; "Baseball is truly tottering on the raw edge of oblivion. Great towns in the North and East are drawing only 1,200 to games now, whereas three or four years ago crowds of 10,000 were not so remarkable."

Ever the optimist, Stanton continued investing in his club and the growing Chattanooga fan base. More work was done at the ball field in anticipation of even larger crowds. Three hundred seats with backs were added for ladies and their male escorts who "found tobacco objectionable." Crews added hitching posts along the sides of the field for tying up previously unrestrained horses. In past years, horses left along the sides of the field would run onto the playing area when hit with a foul ball and the hitching posts brought a welcome end to the unwelcome interruption to the game.

Schoolwork took a back seat to baseball in 1893. Parents sent their boys to school with notes, "asking their sons to be excused from their studies earlier than 3:30 p.m. so they can reach the park before the game started."

According to The Chattanooga Times, the superintendent of schools complied with each request, knowing fully that if he didn't the boys would simply skip school that day all together.

Twelve teams took the field throughout the Southern League in 1893. The Chattanooga club chose a new name – the Warriors – and leapt into the season eager for an earnest pennant victory.

It was not to be.

By July, the Warriors sat in fourth place winning forty-eight of ninety-three games. Despite lagging behind, their level of play was improving hinting at a promising finish to the season. The Warriors fought for a second place finish, or maybe even first. But Mother Nature interrupted.

In late July, yellow fever descended on Pensacola where the New Orleans club just arrived to play ball. Fearful of an epidemic in Chattanooga, city officials placed all people and parcels in and around Pensacola on a 20-day quarantine. Nothing from Pensacola was allowed into Chattanooga until nearly September, including the two ball clubs stranded in the Florida Panhandle.

By the time the quarantine was lifted, the season was over, leaving the Warriors unable to play for a second title.

Interrupted seasons and unfinished play hurt the league in the fans' eyes, and the crowds stayed home the following season. Chattanooga didn't field a team at all and the league – boasting just eight teams – folded for the fourth time in early July.

Eager to maximize his resources, Stanton brought an amateur team to Stanton Field on July 3rd to attempt the first night game ever played in Chattanooga. The clubs played under arc lights to a Chattanooga victory, 9 – 0.

The desperate attempt to draw a crowd to the Stanton House had little affect on the hotel's future. By 1895, the Stanton House proved to be a failed venture – a flash in the proverbial tourist attraction pan. Despite lofty aspirations, crowds that came to East Chattanooga never stayed, preferring the settled and developed downtown along the banks of the Tennessee River.

Baseball hadn't proven to be the crowd-retainer he had hoped for either and the club was a financial burden on a man already struggling to keep his real estate investment afloat.

When investors from Mobile, Alabama crossed the banker's path in 1895, Stanton leapt at the opportunity to unload the team. The Southern League franchise, in town since 1885, left on July

19th, and the ball field behind the Stanton House stood empty. Stanton was out of the baseball business.

After the 1896 season, the Southern League formally dissipated and the South was without professional baseball for the fifth time in eleven seasons.

Chattanooga didn't slow down in baseball's absence. In 1899, the city became home to the first franchised Coca-Cola bottling plant, which still operates in the city today.

Around the turn of the century, talk sprouted again of a revival of professional baseball in the south. In 1900, that talk took shape in the form of the Southern Association.

> **"For the Record"**
>
> August 20, 1914 – Jeff Clark pitched 18 scoreless innings in a doubleheader against Birmingham. The Lookouts claimed the first victory 1-0, while the second game was called at the end of nine innings on account of darkness, both teams still scoreless.
>
> From September 9th to the 14th, in 1915, the Lookouts compiled seven consecutive shutouts with pitchers George Cunningham, "Mudball" Clark, Rube Marshall, and a pitcher named Atkinson, racking up 53 scoreless innings. The club from Mobile, Alabama ended the Lookouts streak on the 15th, serving Chattanooga with two consecutive losses in a doubleheader.
>
> June 13, 1919 – The Lookouts were involved in one of the longest games in Southern League history – 23 innings against the Atlanta Crackers.
>
> June 21, 1940 – The Lookouts claim yet another record of length, playing in the longest night game on record with the Southern League: 20 innings ending in a 7-4 loss to Little Rock.

Abner Powell, Newt Fisher, and Charley Frank decided each team would have twelve players on their roster and they set a salary cap - $1,200 per team per month.

At the start of the Association's first game in 1901, Chattanooga was back in baseball playing alongside Nashville, Little Rock, Memphis, New Orleans, Shreveport, Birmingham, and Selma.

The clubs new owner, Mims Hightower, placed Lew Whistler in charge of the players and Chattanooga claimed a sixth place finish.

In 1902, Selma bowed out but the Atlanta Crackers bid back into the game. Chattanooga claimed another sixth place finish, unable to attract fans or keep the interest of Hightower. The owner sold Chattanooga's franchise to Montgomery in 1903.

For the second time, Chattanooga was without a professional baseball franchise and, like the Southern Association, the city was about to receive a serious facelift.

Representatives from Southern Railway had their eye on the Stanton House, deeming the grounds the perfect place to build a new train station to ease thick crowds at Central passenger station in Chattanooga.

Stanton was all too aware of his failing business venture. Two years later, Southern Railway purchased the hotel along with the twenty-three acres around it, for a bargain price of $71,500 – slightly less than three-quarters the cost Stanton spent to build the hotel thirty-five years earlier.

Chattanooga didn't field a team again until 1909. However, the Lookout City saw some baseball in 1905 when the club from Shreveport came to town to finish the last half of their season, pushed out of Louisiana by yellow fever.

In the spring of 1906, Southern Railway cleared all twenty-three acres and tore the hotel down to the foundation. In its place, they built the Terminal Station – the city's new gateway passenger train station. The terminal operated until August 11, 1970, when Southern Railway closed the doors, boarded the windows, and moved out. Today, the building is home to the Chattanooga Choo Choo Holiday Inn and Convention Center – a prominent tourist attraction featuring a wood-burning locomotive similar to the legendary Chattanooga Choo Choo immortalized in song.

Most of the large bricks used to build the Stanton House were salvaged and, in 1909, used in the construction of Hamilton Bank-founder T.R. Preston's house on Missionary Ridge. The house, now nearly a century old, still stands at 122 N. Crest Road, on Missionary Ridge, boasting walls of brick a foot thick and at least 135 years old.

While the Stanton House was razed and the Preston house and Terminal Station were erected, Southern Railway laid a labyrinth of railroad track across the Chattanooga ball team's longtime playing field.

That same year, Oliver Burnside "O.B." Andrews, son of a Confederate soldier from Yazoo City, Mississippi, and then-owner of Andrews Paper Box Company, took ownership of a franchise in the South Atlantic (Sally) League, and brought the team to play at Chamberlain Field.

It was in 1909 the club earned the team name they bear today, as a result of a fan contest. W.O. Powell suggested the club be known as the Lookouts, pulling from the city's military history and fans approved.

The Single-A ball team – the Lookouts - won the first half of the season while Augusta swept the second, thus facing off to battle for the Sally League title.

When the teams prepared for the pennant playoffs, Augusta kidnapped Chattanooga's pitcher and, reportedly, put something in the Lookout's drinking water.

The series wasn't without incident, Gammon wrote:

"There was much rivalry between Augusta and Chattanooga in 1909. Each time the teams would play, the whole town would go out to the ballpark to see them. Sometimes the game had to stop and let the ballplayers cool off after their fights."

Despite Augusta's efforts to sabotage the games with claims that the Lookouts were fielding players contracted with other teams, the Lookouts won the final game, claimed the pennant, and headed south to Atlanta to play in the Dixie Series.

Led by manager Johnny Dobbs, Chattanooga defeated the Crackers to claim the Dixie Series championship, setting an all-time high win percentage of .695, with eighty-two wins and just thirty-six losses.

The following season, Andrews purchased the Southern Association franchise from Little Rock, Arkansas, with his partner Z.C. Patten, for $12,000 and moved them to Chattanooga. The team moved to a new field a few blocks east of Erlanger Hospital in the 1100 block of East Third Street (then Harrison Avenue) and dubbed it Andrews Field, where they would remain for nearly one hundred years.

That same year, in a bakery in the same town, the now popular Moon Pie – a treat synonymous with life in the South – was born. Both Moon Pies and Lookouts baseball would have a lasting affect on the face of a nation.

Dobbs managed the club in 1910 to a fourth place finish, while Billy Smith took over the helm in 1911 and 1912, claiming fifth and seventh place finishes. In 1913, the most notable Norman Arthur "Tabasco Kid" Elberfeld, one of the hottest tempered players in baseball, was named manager of the Chattanooga Lookouts and legendary baseball began in the Scenic City of the South.

Chapter Three

Ol' Stubblebeard and the Kid

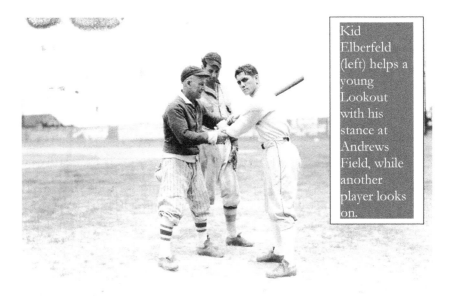

Kid Elberfeld (left) helps a young Lookout with his stance at Andrews Field, while another player looks on.

In 1913, Andrews made a command decision that would alter the course of Lookouts history.

Since 1898, he'd heard of a fiery-tempered ball player they called "The Tabasco Kid" – Norman Arthur Elberfeld.

"Kid," as he was commonly called, played for fourteen seasons, most of which he spent with the New York Highlanders (today's New York Yankees).

The shortstop played a total 1,292 games in his career, swatting a career-high .341 in his first year in New York and was credited with helping the club rise as contenders the following season.

But Elberfeld didn't earn his nickname because he was a "hot" player. Rather, his temper was legendary.

During a game in the minor leagues in Clarkson, Tenn., he was suspended after throwing mud in an umpire's mouth after he was called out. In 1903, the Detroit Tigers traded Elberfeld after he was suspended for again abusing an umpire. Three years later, police had to forcibly remove Kid from the Highlanders playing field during a win over the Philadelphia Athletics, in which Kid yet again assaulted an umpire.

In 1908, then-manager and future Washington Senators owner Clark "the Ol' Fox" Griffith, left the Highlanders, claiming the club wasn't willing to spend the money necessary to build a quality team. At age 33, Elberfeld stepped into the manager's seat and the Highlanders took an 8th place finish – last in the league.

After one more season, the Highlanders parted with Elberfeld, trading him to the Senators where he, once again, played under Griffith until the end of the 1911 season.

In 1912, he took a year off of baseball until Lookouts owner Andrews gave him a call. He needed someone as well connected as Elberfeld to help take his club to the next level and attract high quality players.

Kid fell in love with Chattanooga on a visit and accepted the job, buying an apple orchard on Signal Mountain and dreaming of starting a family.

When the team convened for the start of the 1913 season, Elberfeld was at the helm. Under his watchful eye, Chattanooga bought sixty players, trying to build a legendary ball club.

The team was famously mean, drawing their inspiration from their hotheaded manager. None of the players shied away from a fight with an umpire.

Three pitchers – Harry Coveleskie, Kroh, and Sommers – led the club winning 17 of 21 games on one road trip, each pitcher throwing entire games without relief.

However, Elbefeld's most famous purchase was of a rising 20-year-old Wisconsin spit-ball pitcher, Burliegh Grimes, who would become known as one of the meanest men in baseball, and one of the greatest.

The burly right-hander grew up working at a lumberyard hauling logs for $1 a day. During a day of work, when Grimes was only 11, he was buried under seven ten-foot logs after a horse tripped over a stump and dropped his load. The boy was lifted from beneath the pile without a scratch.

When he was 16, Grimes' father gave him a command and $25 – "Son, go out into the world and make something of yourself."

The teenager wandered for a few years, playing baseball from town to town before Kid found him and brought him to Chattanooga.

In 1913, the burly Burleigh Grimes took the mound for the Lookouts. It may have been Kid's idea that Grimes add to his already intimidating stature by not shaving on the days he played. Regardless, the

Grimes

trick earned the scruffy-faced Grimes his nickname – Ol' Stubblbeard.

The barrel-chested logger also wore his baseball caps a half-size too small, yet another way of making his already large frame seem even larger.

"Brother against Brother" During the 1920 World Series, former Chattanooga Lookout Doc Johnston and his brother, Jimmy, became the first brother to play against brother in a championship game. Jimmy Johnston later served as the Lookouts manager in 1927 and 1929.

Grimes stayed only a single season but helped Kid take Chattanooga from the bottom of the Southern Association to finishing in third place, with a win over Mobile. Atlanta, again, won the pennant.

In the same year, Fred Graf played third base.

"I was what I always called tenacious, not pugnacious. But Elberfeld was always getting thrown out of games," Graf said. "Now, we didn't carry but four or five pitchers and a utility man back then. I told Elberfeld, 'You're always getting thrown out of games and that hurts us. You don't play half the time.'"

Graf played the game when "the infield had to be watered down and was still hard as concrete. Batters were hit by bean balls and pitchers expected to go nine innings.

"You were so glad to be in this game. There was no such thing as walking into the front office midway through the season and demanding more money. They'd throw you out on your ear."

Graf

Graf stayed in Chattanooga for eight years, posting a .265 batting average and becoming one of the most aggressive bunters in the game.

One time, after Grimes left the Lookouts for Birmingham, Graf faced off against Ol' Stubblebeard.

When Grimes decided to intentionally walk Graf, the young Lookout objected. He leaned across the plate and took a solid poke at the very outside pitch. His bat found its mark and Graf earned a single off what Grimes intended to be a walk.

Angry at the batter flipping the tables, Grimes hurled the ball over the grandstand.

In 1915, Graf met his wife, Rea, on a trolley after a Lookouts game. She was "a rabid baseball fan" and convinced Graf to make the Scenic City his home.

He didn't require much convincing.

Graf stayed in Chattanooga the rest of his life, operating the Lookout Billiard Hall, Lookout Recreation Hall, and the Big Four Club for 27 years. He died at age 90 in October 1979.

"I loved baseball and played it for the fun of it," he said. "I never wanted to make a fortune out of it as some of these fellows nowadays do. No managers or agents; just you and a contract with the owner.

"When the good Lord calls me, I'll thank him for a wonderful life – the best anybody ever had."

Grimes was forced to leave Graf and the Lookouts when he broke his leg after the 1914 season.

In 1916, he joined the Birmingham Barons. While there, he gave only 18 hits in 56 innings during six games in late-July and early August. By September, he signed a contract with the Brooklyn Dodgers.

When he reached Brooklyn, everyone was already afraid of him. Brooklyn's team manager, Wilbert Robinson, feared Grimes so much he sent the clubhouse boy to tell Grimes when it was his turn to bat.

Historians credit Grimes orneriness to his days playing for Kid, and it was a reputation Ol' Stubblebeard lived up to.

He was notorious for throwing the first pitch to each new batter directly at their heads. The move intimidated most players, causing them to be so afraid of the next pitches, they would simply stand by the plate hoping not to get hit while the strikes flew by.

Roger Kahn, in his book, <u>Memories of Summer: When Baseball Was an Art, and Writing About It a Game</u>, said of Grimes: "On the sunniest of Flatbush days, Grimes was dour as a hangover."

Some of his most notorious bad days went as follows:

In the fifth game of the 1920 World Series, Grimes became the first pitcher ever to give up a grand slam in the championship game.

In 1925, he became the first player to hit into two double plays and a triple play in a single game.

As manager of the Brooklyn Dodgers in 1937, following a seven-run loss to the Chicago Cubs, Grimes was confronted on the field by a 12-year-old boy star-struck and seeking an autograph from the legendary pitcher. Grimes punched the boy in the stomach.

After that season, he was fired as general manager and replaced by the Sultan of Swat, Babe Ruth. Incidentally, Ruth was replaced the next season after refusing to learn the signals for hit, bumt, run and swing.

However, Grimes highs far outweighed his lows.

He is generally regarded as one of the greatest spitball pitchers of all-time, throwing the last legal spitball in 1934 as a New York Yankee. Grimes won twenty games in five separate seasons in his 17-year career. In 1964, he was inducted into the Hall of Fame.

His first professional baseball coach, Kid Elberfeld, returned to the Majors in 1914, playing with the Brooklyn Robins. In his absence, Harry McCormick led the Lookouts for two years, both to 6th place finishes, until Kid returned to the Lookouts in 1916 and 1917, seeing a 7th and 6th place finish respectively.

In 1918, Elberfeld took a job managing the Southern Association team in Little Rock, where he stayed for several years before partnering with Tubby Walton to start a baseball pitching school in Atlanta in the late 1920s. Pneumonia claimed his life at his Signal Mountain home in 1944 when he was 69.

Grimes outlived his coach by many years, possibly scaring off the Reaper until December 1985, at the age of 92.

With Kid in Little Rock and Grimes gone to the majors, Mike Finn managed the club in 1918, until Sammy Strang Nicklin – the former Sullivan and son of the former Southern Association president – returned from his post as a coach at West Point and bought the Chattanooga Lookouts in 1919. He retained ownership of the club until 1927, and served as manager from 1919 to 1922 and again in 1925 to a string of 6th and 8th place finishes.

The 1923 and '24 seasons saw manager Leslie Nunamaker lead the team.

Elberfeld returned to manage the Lookouts for one more season in 1926, seeing yet another 6th place finish.

That same year, Nicklin and Elberfeld came face to face with another baseball legend and tried their best to break the rules set by strict National Baseball Commissioner Judge Kenesaw Mountain Landis to put a Negro League player into the Lookouts uniform for a single game against rivals, the Atlanta Crackers.

Chapter Four

"Only one person can pitch like me."

Sammy Strang Nicklin and Kid Elberfeld didn't know Leroy Robert Paige spent five years in the Industrial School for Negro Children in Mount Meigs, Alabama.

Satchel Paige, pictured above, playing for the Kansas City Monarchs.

Leroy was the sixth of twelve children born to a gardener and a domestic worker. When he was seven years old, he'd earned the nickname he'd never shake while working as a porter in the Mobile, Alabama, railroad depot.

"I rigged up ropes around my shoulders and waist," Leroy said later. "I carried a satchel in each hand and one under each arm. I carried so many satchels that all you could see was satchels. You couldn't see Leroy Paige."

Despite a work ethic seemingly instilled since birth, Leroy Robert "Satchel" Paige had a knack for truancy.

Early accounts state Paige got into trouble after defending himself against bullies by throwing rocks at their heads from great distances. He got into trouble because of his amazing accuracy, hitting several children spot on.

After facing charges of shoplifting and truancy at the school he regularly attended, Paige, at the tender age of twelve, wound up in Mount Meigs.

During his stay, Satchel Paige focused more on his pitching, encouraged by staff and faculty trying to get the boy to focus on something he was good at other than misbehaving. Over time, he honed his skill into an art form.

By the time the lanky, 6-foot 3-inch, 140 pound Paige left Mount Meigs at seventeen years of age, the sport of baseball consumed him. He returned home to a mother who disapproved of the sport, but he played anyway. In the afternoons of 1924 and 1925, Paige could be found on the mound of a nearby sandlot, playing ball with the Mobile Tigers.

And so it was in such a way, on such a day in 1925, that Alex Herman, a scout for a Negro League baseball team in Chattanooga, found Satchel Paige.

Herman scouted for a series of men, "Bo" Carter, Bud Haley, and W.C. Hixson – a local barber – who owned, from time to time, Negro League teams in Chattanooga.

In 1926, the team was called the Chattanooga White Sox. Negro League teams shared Andrews Field with the neighboring white team – the Lookouts – since 1921, when they called themselves the Tigers under manager Carl Bradley.

It was likely during a game or a practice that a young railroad porter told Herman of a sandlot player he'd seen in Mobile going by the name Satchel Paige.

The boy with size twelve shoes and spot-on accuracy from the mound intrigued Herman, so he made an instant trip to Alabama's port city on the Gulf of Mexico to woo the teenager to professional baseball.

When Herman showed up on Paige's doorstep, Satchel's mother, Tula, sent him away like an ill-intentioned boy trying to court her innocent daughter.

Herman persisted and she refused, certain the footloose life of a baseball player would corrupt her already impressionable son. But one day, money won Tula over, as it often does. The scout promised he'd send every penny of Satchel's $50 monthly salary home to her, and that he would watch over Paige as if her were his own son. The weary mother of 11 other children finally gave in and let her son go to professional baseball.

And go he did.

At 18 years of age, in 1926, the young sandlot pitcher boarded a train in the depot that birthed his nickname, and headed north, bound for greatness.

LEROY ROBERT PAIGE
SATCHEL
NEGRO LEAGUES 1926-1947
CLEVELAND A.L. 1948-1949
ST. LOUIS A.L. 1951-1953
KANSAS CITY A.L. 1965
PAIGE WAS ONE OF THE GREATEST STARS
TO PLAY IN THE NEGRO BASEBALL LEAGUES
THRILLED MILLIONS OF PEOPLE AND WON
HUNDREDS OF GAMES. STRUCK OUT 21 MAJOR
LEAGUERS IN AN EXHIBITION GAME. HELPED
PITCH CLEVELAND INDIANS TO THE 1948
PENNANT IN HIS FIRST BIG LEAGUE YEAR
AT AGE 42. HIS PITCHING WAS A LEGEND
AMONG MAJOR LEAGUE HITTERS

In a 1953 Collier's magazine article, writer Richard Donovan described Paige's debut as a member of the White Sox.

"When he appeared on the Lookouts' field for the first time, the legend-to-be was an arresting sight. His uniform flapped about him. His neck, arms and legs indicated severe emaciation. Spikes had to be nailed to his shoes until some size twelve, triple-A baseball shoes could be found. His walk was labored; he cranked up like the Tin Woodsman of Oz and he appeared to be speechless. Looking at him, veteran players expressed the gravest fears for owner Herman's judgement. The first man to face him in a practice session held his bat in one hand, for charity's sake.

"Then Satchel threw his first ball."

Paige's fastball was legendary.

In 1934, while playing ball in Bismarck, North Dakota, Paige placed a matchbox on a stick next to home plate, then proceeded to knock the matchbox off the stick with twelve of thirteen pitches. With his accuracy established, he then hurled a ball at the catcher, who instantly called for a chest protector and mask. The decision was a good one, as he wasn't able to keep a grip on eight of Paige's next ten throws.

One of the National League's greatest hitters, Hack Wilson, once said Paige's fastball started at the mound the size of a baseball but looked like a marble when it reached the plate. Paige replied, "[He] must be talking about my slow ball. My fastball looks like a fish egg."

Roy Hawes and Satchel Paige as teammates in Miami.

His self-confidence bordered on egotistical but was also legendary, almost from the very beginning of his career.

Paige spent the first year in Chattanooga under Herman's watchful eye. Often, he declined dinner invitations from teammates, stating he'd promised his mother he'd "eat at Mr. Herman's house and go to bed at nine-thirty."

While on the road as a Chattanooga White Sock, hotel desk clerks received scented notes addressed to Paige, while eager, lustful young girls, stood on the sidewalk outside talking to his fellow players.

The lanky ballplayer was upstairs, locked in his hotel room by Herman, left only to look out the window and listen to the voices of his admirers.

"There were times he felt he'd have to jump," Donovan wrote.

So, the 18-year-old earned $50 a month – none of which he ever saw – and lived under arguably more strict guidelines than his time in Mount Meigs, but his love of the game pushed him through and he never lost his pride.

When Nicklin heard of the White Sox teenage hurler, he knew he had to take a peek. After seeing Paige's unique delivery – standing on one leg while leaning the other leg and torso almost horizontal to the ground, then letting loose a lightning bolt pitch with deadly accuracy – he knew this young man needed to pitch for him.

However, strict guidelines established by baseball's most stern commissioner – Judge Kenesaw Mountain Landis – prohibited a Negro from pitching in a white league. But there had to be a way around that edict and, if any player was worth an exception, it was Paige.

The rookie pitcher would be the perfect surprise for the Lookout's upcoming game against their largest rival, the Atlanta Crackers.

So Nicklin, certainly after talking it over with Kid, approached Paige with an offer and a firm belief any man could be bought. He was certain Paige could be persuaded to bend or outright break any rule if the pile of cash in front of him was large enough.

But Nicklin had never met Satchel Paige.

Strang offered Paige $500 – ten times his monthly salary and not a dime of it going to his mother – to play a single game for the Chattanooga Lookouts.

The catch?

No one could know a Negro was playing for the team, so he would have to perform in white face.

Surely, it was the most money Paige had ever seen – ever been offered! Plus, the chance to play against a white team – to out-pitch the white pitchers and strike out some of the rising legends of the white leagues – must have been a draw for the self-assured Satchmo. Even if he were the only one who knew he'd bested some of the white league's elite.

But without hesitation – without even a thought – Paige tossed the chance and the pile of cash to the side. And, in a blink, his legendary wit and brazen self-confidence gleamed through.

"I would look grand in white face," he replied, "but nobody would be fooled … only one person can pitch like me."

Though he declined the offer from the Single A Southern League club, Herman and the club took a hard look at the player they had.

Paige's next season changed drastically off the field, as he was free to dine with the players, fraternize with his female fans, and stay up well after his aforementioned nine-thirty curfew. On the field, it changed too as one of the trio of Negro League owners took over the franchise, renaming them the Chattanooga Black Lookouts.

By the time Paige reached his 21st birthday, he'd owned two roadsters, played guitar with Louis Armstrong, dined with Jelly Roll Martin, and headlined several newspapers in the Negro press.

"It was an education," he told Donovan. "I was tired all the time."

In the middle of the 1927 season, ownership changed hands again and the club was renamed the Chattanooga All-Stars.

By season's end, Paige's celebrity was spreading. Any Negro League player whose skills tempted the manager of a white team in the Southern League to disregard rules set by Landis – a commissioner notorious for barring cheaters from the game – would quickly draw attention from other teams.

When the Birmingham Black Barons came calling at the end of the 1927 season, offering a staggering $275 per month, Paige's interest was peaked. But he finally broke his contract with Chattanooga when the New Orleans Black Pelicans offered him a salary of $200 per month and threw in an antiquated car.

Paige stepped out of Chattanooga and into greatness, pitching for various Negro League teams and, in the off-season, freelancing his services to any group of nine men willing to pay between $500 and $2,000 for three innings of "Satchmo" on the mound.

For two decades, he traveled an average 30,000 miles per year and earned as much as $35,000. His ads stated he was, "Satchel Paige: World's Greatest Pitcher, Guaranteed to Strike Out the First Nine Men."

In the winter, he played games in Jamaica and the Caribbean Islands or he played barnstorming games against major leaguers trying to stay in shape.

He was the star of the Satchel Paige All-Stars, one time out-pitching Dizzy Dean 1-0. He struck out hall-of-fame member and future Chattanooga Lookout coach Rogers Hornsby five times in a single game. Joe DiMaggio stated Paige was "the best and fastest pitcher I've ever faced."

In 1946, when Jackie Robinson became the first black player to break the color barrier in Major League Baseball, Paige waited his turn. When his phone didn't ring at the start of 1948, Paige wondered if his age was playing against him.

In 1926, when Paige started with the Chattanooga White Sox, Joe DiMaggio was 11 years old. When Paige entered Major

League Baseball with the Cleveland Indians, DiMaggio was known as the New York Yankees' "Grand Ol' Man."

In fact, St. Louis Sporting News publisher J.G. Taylor Spink reinforced Paige's sentiments when he editorialized, "many well-wishers of baseball emphatically fail to see eye to eye with the signing of Satchel Paige, superannuated Negro pitcher...To bring in a pitching rookie of Paige's age...is to undermine the standards of baseball in the big circuits."

That season, in front of record crowds of nearly 80,000 people, Paige lost only one of seven games, boasted a 2.47 ERA, and led the Indians to a pennant win. Many sports writers voted Paige to be the Rookie of the Year.

But Paige declined.

"I wasn't sure which year the gentlemen had in mind," he said.

He played more than 2,500 games in his lifetime, averaging 125 games each year. Historians say Paige won about 2,000 games – claiming 250 shutouts and 45 no-hitters and, in 1935, pitched 29 consecutive days with only one loss.

At age 59, in 1965, he retired as a player from the game. He continued a few years later as a coach for the Atlanta Braves.

On August 9, 1971, Paige became the first Negro League player to be inducted into the National Baseball Hall of Fame in Cooperstown, New York.

In his 75 years of life, he was most famous for his wit, despite a lack of formal education.

During a practice wit the Cleveland Indians, while some of the players were jogging and Paige sat in the bullpen reading a book, they started to tease him, calling, "Ain't you gonna run? Ain't you gonna get in shape?"

He replied, matter-of-factly, "No, where I come from we throw the ball across the plate, we don't carry it across."

Though a heart attack caused his death at his Kansas City home in 1982, everyone knew the impact of his legendary life.

Former Negro Leaguer, Buck O'Neil, said, "See, Satchel did to black baseball what Ruth did to white baseball … Ruth kept the franchises going. [Paige] is the guy that the people wanted to see. And he never failed."

Dizzy Dean noted Paige's showmanship, saying, "If Satch and I was pitching on the same team, we'd clinch the pennant by the fourth of July and go fishing until World Series time."

As time would prove, another great showman would arrive in Chattanooga on the heels of young Satchel's departure as the game of baseball reorganized and as the nation faced its largest economic slump.

<u>Chapter</u> <u>Five</u>

The Circus Comes to Town

While Kid Elberfeld rallied the Lookouts in 1916, a young man named Branch Rickey prepared to change the face of baseball and ultimately bring the major league to Chattanooga.

Prior to 1901, all Minor League Baseball teams played in unrelated leagues. In the fall of that year, the two existing baseball leagues – the National and the American – agreed to join forces and create the National Association of Professional Baseball Leagues.

At that point, Minor League Baseball teams were organized into leagues. By 1949, Minor League Baseball hosted 59 leagues featuring 464 teams drawing 42 million fans out to the ballgame each year. At that point, minor league ball teams were not affiliated with major league teams. Instead, they were viewed as simply breeding grounds – training camps – for potential major league stars.

By now, baseball was a business as well as a game. Owners contracted players who played for salaries – meager, to say the least – but salaries just the same. If, for instance, the owner of a major league ball team wanted to purchase a shortstop for their team, they would simply place a call to their nearest minor league club and "shop" for the best player. When they found a player they wanted, the major league team would buy the players' contract – a price arbitrarily set by the minor league club owner.

Major league teams with little money to spend were at a disadvantage. Once one minor league club caught wind of a major league team shopping for a certain player – say, a shortstop – the news scattered through the minors from clubhouse to clubhouse like lightning in a high desert thunderstorm. Before the sun set on that same day, the asking price of all shortstops among all minor league teams had gone up.

Teams with little money to spend were at the mercy of a player's bidding war and, often times, couldn't compete. They were forced to accept lower caliber players for less money while marquis players went to wealthy clubs with the extra cash to spread around.

Branch Rickey, then head of the debt-ridden St. Louis Cardinals, later recalled "necessity (was) the mother of invention."

"Starting the Cardinals farm system was no sudden stroke of genius. We lived a precarious existence. Other clubs would outbid us; they had the money and the superior scouting systems. We had to take the leagues or nothing at all."

So, in 1919, Rickey and the Cardinals started purchasing controlling interest – or outright buying – struggling minor league teams throughout the nation. Initially, most major league team owners, when hearing of Rickey's actions, wrote him off as completely insane.

But the Cardinals kept purchasing and, over time, compiled a network of minor league teams he could "farm" for new players. Since the Cardinals owned the teams, each player was a contracted player for the St. Louis Cardinals organization, meaning whenever Rickey found a player he deemed worthy of the majors, he didn't need to by their contract – he already owned it! Instead, the player simply packed a bag and took a step into the majors.

Along with saving bags of cash, the Cardinals could offer individual attention and guidance to promising athletes, ensuring strong teams down the road.

Rickey's plan worked, despite blooming under a cloud of skepticism from his peers. By 1942, the St. Louis Cardinals stated a definite case for this new way of conducting business. The organization had grown to include 800 players across thirty-two teams, all of whom helped the Cardinals clinch six division pennants, four Word Series, and a permanent place at the top of the league standings for more than twenty years.

After a decade of watching the St. Louis Cardinals gain strength in the majors as they bolstered numbers in the minors, a sly and cunning ex-ballplayer turned his attention on Chattanooga.

Clark "the Ol' Silver Fox" Griffith owned the Washington Senators and had since 1912, when he mortgaged his Montana ranch for enough money to buy a small portion of the club. The Silver Fox was former pitcher, playing with various clubs – the St. Louis Browns, Boston Reds, Chicago Colts, Chicago Orphans, Chicago White Stockings, New York Highlanders, Cincinnati Reds, and the Senators – from 1891 to 1914. He threw six consecutive twenty-victory seasons and led the White Stockings to win the first American League pennant in 1901. Through his twenty-four seasons on the mound, he tallied 237 career wins.

When he shifted his focus to the business side of baseball in the mid-1910s, the Fox was equally successful.

"He Wears a White Hat"
When rookie first baseman Roy Hawes reported to Clark Griffith's office for his first trip to the majors in September 1951, he had to wait.

The clock in the lobby read 1 p.m. and the door to Griffith's office was closed. As one o'clock turned into a quarter after, the receptionist confided no one was with Griffith in his office. He was listening to his favorite half-hour radio program, The Lone Ranger.

"She told me he never missed the show and he never took visitors during the broadcast," Hawes said.

Promptly at 1:30 p.m., when the show ended, the door opened and Hawes was ushered in. He almost couldn't believe what he saw.

"The office was full of Lone Ranger memorabilia and there was a picture of Griffith with Clayton Burrows, who played the Lone Ranger," he said.

Hawes story begs the question: Was Joe Engel the Tonto to Griffith's Lone Ranger?

Maybe so, Kimosabe. Maybe so.

a

Griffith took over as manager of the Senators in 1912, immediately going to work putting together a championship team. With future hall-of-fame pitcher Walter Johnson on the roster, Griffith and the Senators finished in second place in 1912 and 1913. In 1924, the Senators claimed the World Series Championship and, the next season, repeated as American League Champions.

From 1926 to 1932, the Senators finished lower than fourth place only once and, in 1933, claimed a third American League title with a record 99 wins in 152 games!

It was at the beginning of the Senators seven-year win streak that Griffith came to Chattanooga. Though he'd spent a quarter century playing baseball in six different cities on eight teams, Griffith found a home in Washington and wanted to give the Senators his best.

He was on the hunt for a good minor league partner for his major league club and found what he sought in the Lookouts. In 1928, the Senators became the major league affiliate of the Chattanooga club and changed the face of Scenic City baseball forever.

The following year, construction began on a new baseball stadium on the site of Andrews Field. The towering park played host to 12,000 seats under sprawling awnings stretching down

"Fine with Me"
A sign painted on the wall down the third base line was directed specifically to the players, reading, "$5 FINE for batting toward the stands."

both base lines. The left field wall stood 325 feet from home plate and the right at 318 feet. However, the centerfield wall demanded national attention, stretching a record 471 feet from home plate – making it the deepest centerfield wall in the history of the game.

At the apex of left and centerfield, an incline donned the word "LOOKOUTS" in bold, white lettering in fair territory, along with a flagpole bearing Old Glory.

Perched high atop the stadium was the press box, built on top of the wide roof. The stadium was one of the first in the country to be built with a press box. Eight ticket windows bordered the main gate and the concourse beneath the stands featured, among other things, a deli! For those who were interested, a barber chair also stood in the bleachers offering a quick shave and a haircut to those attending the game.

The Fox had found the perfect city for his club, choosing Chattanooga over Atlanta because of its proximity to Washington. The Lookouts' players were eager to join the ranks of the Senators organization and the newly constructed green giant at the corner of O'Neal and East Third streets proved a patient host.

"Picky Rickey" Branch Rickey – attributed with forming the minor league farm system while he owned the St. Louis Cardinals and breaking baseball's color line by bringing Jackie Robinson to the majors while managing the Brooklyn Dodgers – visited Engel Stadium in 1953.

After taking a private tour of all the stadium had to offer, Rickey said the park was "most exceptional in efficiency."

All that remained was to choose a leader for this new venture – a liaison between Washington and Chattanooga, major and minor. A man who would orchestrate the induction of major league baseball prospects into the Scenic City of the South and become the namesake of the record setting baseball stadium.

Griffith found that leader in an old friend, Joseph William Engel.

Born in Washington, D.C. in 1893, Engel was one of six children born to a German immigrant who owned a string of hotels in D.C. Engel was raised at the ballpark and spent his youth playing with Kermit and Alice Roosevelt, President Teddy Roosevelt's children.

He was a Senators batboy and, later, served as the team mascot. In college, he lettered in four sports – track, baseball, basketball, and football. Pursuing his passion for baseball, he tried to make it as a pitcher in the majors from 1912 to 1920, playing for Washington five of his seven career seasons.

In his first year in the majors, he roomed with future hall-of-famer, Walter Johnson.

"People used to wonder at our close friendship – said we were so different," Engel recalled. "Walter didn't drink or smoke and was more or less on the serious side. I liked my fun and as a youngster was something of a hell-raiser. But we just clicked."

As a player, the young Engel was mediocre, playing in 407 games and starting only 40. Of those, Engel won only 17 games and posted a career ERA of 3.38. In three of his seven playing seasons, he appeared in a single game each year. He still holds a claim to contributing to the single-game record for most batters hit by a pitch.

While pitching wasn't his strong suit, Engel had a knack for spotting natural athletic talent. All too aware of his own limitations, Engel chose to focus on his strengths, hanging up his cleats in 1920. Griffith hired Engel as a scout in 1920, a move the Ol' Fox nearly regretted.

In the early 1920s, Griffith sent Joe to report on a rising prospect named Paul Strand. Engel quickly reported the boy would "never make it in the majors" and advised Griffith to pass him up, which Griffith did.

A few years later, a budding Strand had come into his own, and sports reporters called Strand a late bloomer whose greatness would likely compare with Babe Ruth and Ty Cobb. The Philadelphia Athletics purchased Strand for $100,000 and brought him to Washington to face off against the Senators, and the man who advised he would never make it to the big leagues, in a preseason exhibition game.

Fearful of being humiliated in front of Griffith by this missed opportunity, Engel headed straight for his buddy, Walter Johnson, to plead his case.

Engel begged Johnson to throw the heat against this reported phenomenon at the plate – to strike Strand out and save his reputation. Johnson responded, in that seemingly meaningless exhibition, by pitching playoff-worthy pitches to Strand and sending the young batter back to the dugout four consecutive times.

Griffith and Engel

In a blink of the Silver Fox's eyes, Engel's scouting career was saved. He went on to bring some of the Senators best players to the club through the next six years, including Joe Cronin, Bucky Harris, Ossie Bluege, Buddy Myer, Doc Prothro, and Goose Goslin.

When Engel first spotted Cronin playing in Kansas City, "I knew I was watching a great player. I bought Cronin at a time he was hitting . 221. When I told Clark Griffith what I had done, he screamed, "You paid $7,500 for that bum? Well, you didn't buy him for me. You bought him for yourself. He's not my ballplayer –he's yours. You keep him and don't either you or Cronin show up at the ballpark."

Cronin would lead the Senators to an American League championship in 1933 and marry Griffith's adopted daughter, to become the owner's son-in-law.

Engel spent his off-season touring the Vaudeville circuit from 1926 to 1929, acting as the manager and narrator in a pantomime boxing act in the same show as budding crooner, Bing Crosby.

Though he picked up a lot of tips of how to entertain while on the road for those three years, setting an attendance record in a Salt Lake City theater, Engel's first love was always baseball.

When the Fox needed to choose someone to head up operations over his newly acquired farm club in Chattanooga, his ace scout was the obvious choice.

However, Engel was in for an uphill battle.

Nearing the completion of construction at Engel Stadium, in October 1929, the stock market crashed and the nation's economy dipped into a tailspin.

Nationally, game attendance plummeted to a 25-year low, forcing some teams to suspend play temporarily. The Negro Leagues suffered such losses in attendance and advertising, they were forced to disband completely. Attendance at games in Chattanooga skirted around 78,000 for the year.

Millions didn't have the half-dollar to spend on admission to the park. A select few opted to skip meals the rest of the day just to come up with enough money for admission and a hotdog at the game. The St. Louis Browns saw less than 1,500 fans coming to the games while the Cincinnati Reds, Philadelphia Athletics, and Boston Braves teetered on the brink of bankruptcy.

Amidst a nations' turmoil, Joe Engel came to Chattanooga and took up his 34-year reign at 1130 East Third Street as one of the most notoriously eccentric promoters in all baseball.

<u>Chapter</u> <u>Six</u>

The King of Baseball

Engel, the self-proclaimed king of baseball.

In his new role as the owner of the Lookouts, at a time when attendance was scraping an all-time low, Joe Engel proved himself a phenomenal promoter.

He knew in order to spike fan interest, he'd have to offer more than a baseball game to a nation full of unemployment and despair. He had to offer entertainment, a sense of prosperity, and hope.

Boy, did he ever.

First and foremost, Engel offered the city her first look at the new stadium in the most unconventional of ways. During the winter of 1929, following the stock market crash, Engel opened the doors to Engel Stadium to feed the poor and hungry affected by the Great Depression. That winter, he fed 11,000 Chattanoogans. The following year, 9,000 turned out for a chance to eat and, in 1931, 7.500 came out for a bite to eat. At Christmas time, Engel used the stadium as a warehouse to hold 7,500 Walter Johnson baseball board games, which he distributed to Chattanooga children who might not otherwise have seen any gift on Christmas morning.

Beyond Christmas morning, Engel continued to care about the well-being of Chattanooga's children.

In 1925, Judge William McGaughy and the Central YMCA organized a baseball club called the Knothole Gang, based on an idea McGaughy gleaned from a St. Louis Cardinal's game. The gang offered school-aged boys the chance to play baseball against other schools as long as they maintained good grades and regular attendance at school and Sunday School at the church of their choosing. Active members of the Knothole Gang also received free admission to most Lookouts baseball games.

When Engel arrived in 1929, he maintained the tradition of the Knothole Gang, adding a special seating section for the club in the new stadium.

Turning his attention to the field, Engel reached into his pockets and picked up the phone in search of any resource he could use to draw a crowd to the park.

Chattanooga had rarely seen a major league club pass through the Scenic City since the day clubs used the field at Douglas and Vine as spring training in the 1880s. Engel and Griffith collaborated to bring the Washington Senators to Engel Stadium to play against the Lookouts in a season-opening exhibition game.

Though the Lookouts took a 3 – 0 loss to their parent affiliate on March 23, 1930, the stadium played host to 2,500 fans –

enough to start the word of mouth about the amazing facility to spread around town.

Fan attendance in 1930 nearly doubled as 146,000 people came to the park for a game. In 1931, the numbers went up again, drawing 172,000 people to the old ball game.

Engel's compassion flowed for his city and her people but the former player displayed some business, some sarcasm, and a lot of humor on the field.

When Griffith made the decision to affiliate with Chattanooga instead of Atlanta, the Cracker's fans responded with smug indignation.

Fans posted signs in their park reading, "The hell with Joe Engel" and "What do we care for Joe Engel and Clark Griffith? We have 14 millionaires."

At the Lookouts' first game against Atlanta, at Atlanta, in 1930, Engel responded. He drove an old jalopy around the edge of the outfield dressed in a battered stove pipe hat and frayed swallow-tail coat, with a sign hanging from the driver's door reading, "Chattanooga's Only Millionaire."

The rivalry between the Lookouts and the Crackers was fierce.

Engel once paid pitcher Charles "Buck" Morrow $100 for every scoreless inning he pitched against the Crackers during a doubleheader. Reportedly, Morrow snared several hundred dollars, paid after each inning, before the other team finally scored a run.

"Sign of the Times" A sign once hanging in Engel's office read, "For when the One Great Scorekeeper comes to write against your life, He writes not that you won or you lost, but how you played the game."

During most games, Engel perched on the top of the stadium roof, standing high above the crowd like the "King of All Baseball" he claimed to be. One umpire once dethroned Engel, kicking him off the roof and out of the game due to verbal jabs Engel rained down at the official from high above.

Ol' Joe was notorious for his run-ins with umpires.

One day when an umpire called a game because of darkness in what Engel perceived to be broad daylight, he sent a wire to the league president (which he also made public) reading, "Suggest a rule be passed no umpires can have dates until 9 p.m." According to lore, it was months before one of the umpires could convince his spouse that the telegram was yet one more of Engel's stunts.

In the 1940s, Lookouts radio broadcaster Tom Nobles got into a street fight with umpire Augie Guglielmo, over remarks on the air concerning Augie's eyesight. Engel immediately reacted to the news of his broadcaster's actions, giving Nobles a three-day vacation with pay.

"It would have been a week if you had licked him," Engel told Noble.

While Engel was tough on umpires, he was equally demanding of his players. He didn't tolerate players who refused to perform, notorious for selling players unable to keep their batting averages above .300.

In 1931, the club's shortstop Johnny Jones wasn't performing up to Engel's standards. When the Charlotte Hornets, the minor league club in Charlotte, North Carolina, came calling for the player, Engel was quick to sell. However, the shortstop drew a unique asking price.

Joe sold Jones for a 25-pound Thanksgiving turkey, stating simply, "the turkey was having a better year." Later, Engel said, "I still think I got the worst of that deal. That was a mighty tough turkey."

Consequently, a turkey sandwich bearing the player's name was served at the ballpark for years thereafter.

While undergoing contract negotiations with another player, Engel's sarcastic humor beamed like the sun. Yet another shortstop was holding out for more money. The player sent a Western Union telegram to Engel stating, "Pay me $5,000 or count me out."

Engel's telegram reply was simple and straight to the point.

"One, Two, Three, Four, Five, Six, Seven, Eight, Nine, Ten."

Engel's greatest promotion was on deck.

Always horsing around, Engel hosted an annual dinner for umpires. Here, each ump wears sunglasses faking blindness.

Chapter Eight

Mocking Murderer's Row

Heads turned, jaws dropped, and time seemingly stood still each time Babe Ruth stepped near a ballpark. Almost every swing of his bat was newsworthy.

But the day the Sultan of Swat swung his bat in Chattanooga turned out to be legendary.

Ruth stepped to the plate at the corner of East Third Street and O'Neal on April 2nd, 1931. But this story began years earlier with the rise of a hall-of-fame pitcher, the competitive drives of two baseball legends, and one little girl.

*   *   *

In the warm summer breezes of 1927, George Herman "Babe" Ruth and Lou Gehrig had a record-setting season swinging bats for the New York Yankees. The pair hit a combined total 107 homeruns – Ruth smacking 60 in a single season, to set the record later broken by Roger Maris, and again by Mark McGwire. Gehrig socked 47 homers beyond the reach of outfield walls. This pair of pin-striped powerhouses were so deadly at the plate, fans dubbed their portion of the New York Yankees' batting order "Murderer's Row".

Though both were living legends, Ruth and Gehrig were in constant competition well into the 1930s. Gehrig was forever living and working in the shadows of the Great Bambino. Sportswriters said he lacked showmanship – something Ruth seemed to simply exude from his pores. They claimed Gehrig didn't swagger the same way Ruth did when he walked, and his homeruns didn't seem to soar quite as high or long as Babe's. Yankees' management, disturbed over Gehrig's lack of headlines, even encouraged him to leap for catches that he knew were impossible to make or to pretend plays were harder than they really were, just to drum up an act that was pleasing to the press and the fans. In short, they wanted him to act more like Ruth.

Gehrig shrugged their request, explaining he simply wasn't "a headline guy."

As the pair kept chasing records season after season, Gehrig began to outpace Ruth, leading the American League in homeruns in 1930. Despite Gehrig's impressive performance, it still wasn't enough to lure the spotlight of national attention away from Ruth and toward himself.

The competition for media attention turned to animosity between the two and, before long, a long and awkward silence settled between the teammates that lasted the better part of a decade.

Ken Burns recounts, in his documentary entitled, Baseball that, "the two men were growing increasingly distant – Gehrig believed Ruth had said something disparaging about his mother …"

So, in the spring of 1931, when the New York Yankees stopped in Chattanooga to play an exhibition game against the semi-pro Chattanooga Lookouts the competition between these two men was fierce and in full swing. One had to be better than the other. National media demanded it. There was no room in the headlines for both, so all eyes were on Ruth and Gehrig, on and off the field, constantly analyzing who was better than whom – whom was stronger, or faster, and which would leave the game as a permanent legend.

No chance to shame a pitcher could be overlooked by either man – the press was always watching, waiting to report any sign of weakness in either man, desperately searching for the Achilles' heel in either man's play.

Neither man could take any game for granted. Every opportunity to hit yet another impressive homerun – to earn that much coveted recognition as the more fierce half of the duo that made up "Murderer's Row" – had to be pursued with passion.

On this day, April 2nd, 1931, within the comforting walls of Engel Stadium, Gehrig would have the chance of a lifetime to take a seat above the mighty Ruth, when the pair faced the most surprising of adversaries; Virnett "Jackie" Mitchell, a 17-year-old, unassuming, blonde.

Left to Right – Lou Gehrig, Jackie Mitchell, Joe Engel, and Babe Ruth talk at Engel Stadium, April 2nd, 1931, after the now unforgettable game.

Born premature, just four pounds at birth, some described her as a sickly child. Doctors encouraged her to get outside and get plenty of exercise.

Mitchell, who lived just down the street from Engel Stadium at 2508 E. Fourth Street, was the student of a hall of fame pitcher who spent the better part of his 15-year career as a Brooklyn Dodger.

Arthur "Dazzy" Vance had a list of accomplishments following his name. In 1921, when Mitchell was seven years old living in Memphis, Tennessee, the then-minor leaguer coached Mitchell in all the aspects of pitching. Three years later, Vance entered the majors as the National League's Most Valuable Player, for which he received $1,000 paid in gold coins. By 1928, he was the highest paid pitcher in baseball, earning $25,000 per year.

The "Dazzler's" fast-pitch blew by a veritable laundry list of baseball's greatest hitters, including the equally egotistical Rogers Hornsby. Though Vance pushed strike three past 2,045 hitters in his major league career, he was more popularly known for his nearly unparalleled ego and his own knack for showmanship.

Tricking batters was almost a hobby for Dazzy. Often, he would cut the sleeve of his shirt on his pitching arm, clear up the seam to the elbow. Then, when he'd hurl the small, white baseball, batters were blinded by a streak of fluttering white fabric drowning out the blue afternoon skies. By the time they separated the ball from the background, it had sailed past them for the shocking strike three.

That was Vance's firmest belief – "The unexpected pitch is still the best pitch anyone can throw." It was a lesson he taught to many budding pitchers, and a lesson Jackie Mitchell would prove to be true when she would take the mound to stare down "Murderer's Row".

Standing on top of the hill in the center of the infield, the 17-year-old was likely all too aware of Dazzy's advice. Also fresh on her mind could have been a need to settle a score with the unbeatable Yankees – to vindicate her mentor from a hole of his own creation.

In the middle of the 1928 season, when Mitchell was stumbling into her teenage years, Vance faced the New York

Yankees only one year after Ruth and Gehrig's record-setting homerun season. Touring a cousin through the hotel lobby filled with Yankee players the night before the game, Vance introduced each player in his own abrasive, self-confident manner.

He went through the players, one by one, describing to his cousin how he – the highest paid pitcher in the game – would take each hitter out the following day.

"Meet Babe Ruth," Vance said. "He'll break his bat swinging at my stuff!"

The next day, with bruised pride and something to prove, the Yankees stepped into the batter's box.

Five of the first six batters hit no less than a double. Ruth sent Dazzy's pitch beyond the outfield wall and Gehrig, "The Iron Horse," walloped Vance's pitch for a triple. After the first six batters, and the Yankees' 5-0 lead on the game in the first inning and only a single out, Vance was sent to the showers.

Along with swallowing five pitches slammed back down his throat that day, Vance also had to eat his pride, as the cousin remarked that was "the easiest way to make $25,000 [he'd] ever seen."

And so, present and past collided on a single stage in a little Southern city in the spring of 1931 – one sunrise after April Fool's Day. Gehrig and Ruth, both with egos to defend and reputations to uphold, viewed this exhibition as earnestly as they would the final game of a pennant race.

Jackie Mitchell, the apprentice of a humbled hall-of-famer, on the edge of her own potentially dazzling career, took her place in the bullpen at Engel Stadium.

Joe Engel found the left-handed pitcher in Georgia at a baseball camp operated by former Lookouts manager Kid Elberfeld and inked a contract with her to play for the Chattanooga Lookouts. Engel was constantly looking for a new attraction to draw fans to the ballpark and, in Mitchell, he believed he'd found it.

Mitchell had less auspicious goals.

"All I want to do is stay in baseball long enough to get money to buy a roadster," she said.

The day the Yankees came to town, making their way north after spring training in Florida, Engel billed Mitchell as the only female pitcher in all of Minor League Baseball, hoping to draw already fiscally-conservative fans to the ballpark in the midst of the Great Depression.

Engel couldn't have had any idea his attempt to spike ticket sales would result in one of the most memorable days in baseball history.

More than 4,000 turned out to the stadium that day, drawn to see a teenage girl try her luck at slinging at least one, much less three, strikes past the unstoppable "Murderer's Row."

The game was originally slated for April Fool's Day but was delayed due to rain. Engel drew criticism from writers of "The Sporting News" for his choice of game day, as they wired him messages such as, "What is Chattanooga trying to do? Burlesque the game?"

But Mitchell was no slouch on the mound, heralded by The Chattanooga News Free Press as having, "control. She can place the ball where she pleases, and her knack at guessing the weakness of a batter is uncanny."

At the start of the game, Mitchell watched from the bullpen while manager Bert Niehoff sent Clyde Barfoot to the mound. However, after Barfoot gave up a double and a base-hit to the first two batters, Niehoff pulled Barfoot and called Mitchell to take the mound.

As she crossed to the infield hill, Babe Ruth stood idly by preparing for his turn to bat. Mitchell's first professional pitch would be to a baseball legend.

100 Seasons of Lookouts Uniforms

The Lookouts uniform has changed many times in the past 100 seasons, alternating style – from block lettering across the chest to just the logo – and many color combinations – red and white, orange and brown, and blue and gold.

And her first pitch was a ball.

The expectant fans surely weren't surprised. After all, Barfoot gave up base hits to otherwise nameless members of the Yankee line-up. What could this teenage girl possibly expect to achieve when pitching to the current single-season homerun record holder, The Great Bambino? Of course her first pitch sagged too low and outside! She'd surely want to keep her pitches as far away from that bat as possible! The next three pitches were almost certain to do the same.

One writer, penning an article that appeared the morning of the game in The New York Daily News, prematurely discredited Mitchell as no more than a circus side-show – "[Today] The Yankees will meet a club that has a girl pitcher … who has a swell change of pace and swings a mean lipstick. I suppose in the next town the Yankees enter they will find a squad that has a female impersonator in left field, a sword-swallower at short, and a trained seal behind the plate. Times in the South are not only tough but silly."

On this day, Dixie truly proved it's fun to watch a Yankee eat his words.

A resolute Jackie wound up for her second pitch, shooting another of her trademark "side-armed sinkers" across the plate. It hugged the outside corner of the plate and Ruth gave a hearty swing, obviously eager to punch a pitch beyond the deepest center field wall in professional baseball.

But he missed it.

Mitchell – the one-dimensional pitcher discovered at a baseball camp in Georgia – leveled the count at one and one against a baseball phenomenon.

Certainly, some fans and players were surprised. Likely, most were surprised that bouncing, blonde curls sneaked a pitch past The Sultan of Swat. Surely, most credited the pitch to luck or Ruth's abounding grace. He must have let her have that one or a bead of sweat must have got in his eye. Something must have affected Ruth in some way in order for a teenage girl to push a pitch past his powerful swing. He was too good to succumb to the pitching prowess of a minor league princess.

Even Mitchell was a little surprised by the pitch.

But when she slipped strike two past Ruth's mighty bat, everyone in the stadium took note.

The second strike edged past the swaggering Sultan and he swung wildly at it. Skeptics became optimists. The first strike was almost definitely luck – but a second? The teenage girl took the upper hand in the count – a daunting one and two for the Babe. Fans could only see this as a dare – a pompous threat made against a baseball great by a virtual no-name girl who came to play big league ball in a small Southern city.

Likely, the stands buzzed with stunted conversation – some questioning the nerve of the new comer and others defending The Great Bambino.

"He's sure to send it out of the park now."

"He won't let her see strike three."

Most importantly, though seemingly unnoticed, an eager, interested, and competitive Lou Gehrig must have sat perched at the edge of the bench, leaning close toward the field, breathlessly waiting to see if his greatest rival would fall to the pitches of a seemingly unassuming girl.

Ruth had once been quoted as saying women would never make it playing professional baseball because "they're too delicate to endure playing baseball every day."

Unfortunately for Ruth, Mitchell needed only to last a single pitch longer in order to leave her mark on history.

No one will ever know what the Babe was thinking at that exact moment. Whether he was equally bewildered by strike two, as some members of the crowd surely were, or if he was fighting off the embarrassment of swinging at two pitches and coming up empty both times.

Regardless of the topic, one thing is for certain – the Babe wasn't watching the mound. As he stood at the plate, Mitchell hurled her fourth pitch – a sinking strike scraping the outside of the plate which caught The Great Bambino standing for strike three.

Without question, the crowd was motionless, save for the possible devoted local fans cheering for the amazing feat they'd just witnessed by this female up-start.

Visibly disgusted – no question with himself, the umpire, and his surprising adversary – Ruth kicked the dirt and threw his bat down onto the plate, staring at the umpire in disbelief. After a short argument, he stalked unhappily back to the dugout.

"[Ruth] looked disgusted, on his face," Mitchell recalled, years later, "and he threw the bat down after the umpire called him out. He didn't like that."

Her heart must have sang, having sent the mighty Ruth back to the bench on her first professional appearance. Even more startled must have been Joe Engel, who, according to National Baseball Hall of Fame Researcher Amanda Pinney, supposedly told the Yankees not to hit the ball back up the middle at Jackie.

Ruth never got the chance to hit the ball back up the middle. Her pitches never touched his bat. Engel's promotional gimmick had put three strikes past the legendary swing of one of baseball's all-time greatest hitters.

And the other half of "Murderer's Row" was stepping to the plate.

Lou Gehrig, "The Iron Horse," was a phenomenon in his own right. He'd proved putting a ball anywhere near the plate could prove fatal to any pitcher's career.

But Mitchell was not unnerved when Gehrig sauntered to the plate, bat in hand. She'd calmed down one pitch earlier.

"After I threw the second strike, I settled down a little," she remembered, in an interview she gave decades later. "I figured then that it wasn't going to be so hard for me to get the ball over the plate."

Now, facing the second pin-striped powerhouse, Mitchell's confidence was high. She'd just knocked down a giant. All she had left to do was make glue out of an Iron Horse.

Gehrig new the headlines tomorrow would read, "Teenage Girl Puts Three Past Ruth" or "Sultan of Swat Strikes Out to 17-year-old Girl" – yet another story he wouldn't headline. But he was confident somewhere near the top of the story people would read how he knocked the next pitch over the outfield wall.

The pair faced off, Gehrig squaring his stance as Mitchell went into her windup. Mitchell's "odd, side-armed delivery ... [putting] both speed and curve on the ball," according to The Chattanooga News, prompted Gehrig to respond with a mighty swing just as the ball sunk low and smacked into the catcher's mitt.

Without doubt, Mitchell was gathering the crowd's favor. Her last four pitches had whizzed past two of the greatest hitters in the history of the sport.

His pride on the line and the crowd shifting to cheer the new pitcher, rather than the visiting slugger, Gehrig buckled down – focusing on the second pitch.

Strike two sailed past Gehrig's streaking bat, sinking low at the last second and settling snug into the catcher's mitt.

Ruth, at least, saw one ball and was forced to sit down after four pitches. Gehrig refused to be sent back to the dugout with three unanswered strikes. He specifically refused to take strike three standing, as Ruth had done. At this point, he would settle for a double, or a short hit for a single. Simply making contact with the ball, even if it mean fouling the ball off just to stay alive for a fourth pitch to tie Ruth's stand against the girl pitcher, would be good enough. He didn't have to hit a homerun but Gehrig simply refused to go down standing.

He didn't.

The Iron Horse went down swinging.

Mitchell slid a third sinker over the plate and past the rushing winds of Gehrig's determined, desperate final swing as the umpire let out a resolute, "Strike three!"

In seven pitches, Jackie Mitchell secured a spot in history under the warm Tennessee sunshine. She stayed in the game for only one more batter – five more pitches – to Tony Lazzeri who, after trying to bunt, was walked. Mitchell was sent back to the bullpen for the remainder of the game, which the Yankees eventually won 14 to 4.

Those seven pitches drew the attention of a nation. Only days after Mitchell's face-off with "Murderer's Row," Commissioner Landis, voided Mitchell's contract with the Chattanooga Lookouts, forbidding her from playing professional baseball again.

His justification?

Landis claimed the game was "too strenuous" for women to play. Many hailed this to be an overreaction at the least and at most, a gross attempt to place a bandage on the bruised machismo's of a few of baseball's legends.

Landis, the same commissioner who banned eight players – including Shoeless Joe Jackson –, from ever playing baseball again after they were accused of betting on their own team, once said, "Baseball is more than a game to an American boy. It is his training field for life work. Destroy his faith in its squareness and honesty and you have destroyed something more; you have planted suspicion of all things in his heart."

While Landis attempted to protect the game for the future generations of aspiring male athletes, he couldn't prevent the spread of Mitchell's accomplishment in barber shops across the nation.

Outside the stadium waited a nation full of cynics and critics, some armed with a pen, who immediately began the debate about whether the pitches were heroism or hoax.

Initially suspect was the original date of the game, April 1, 1931 – April Fool's Day. Mitchell was slated to play against the Yankees on this day for practical jokes but the game was rained out and rescheduled. Was Mitchell nothing more than a clown for the notorious practical joker and promotional mastermind, Joe Engel?

Some proposed Engel arranged for the Yankee sluggers to strike out, in an effort to spike fan attendance at the ballpark during a national recession.

Mitchell refuted the doubters until her dying day in 1987.

"Why, hell yes, they were trying, damn right," she said. "Hell, better hitters than them couldn't hit me…Why should they've been any different?

"To me, it's like a dream now, more than a reality. At the time I didn't think it would go as far as it has. I liked [Ruth and Gehrig] both – I enjoyed talking to both of them but Lou Gehrig was a bit nicer. He was more friendlier. Ruth was quiet and didn't have much to say."

Tony Lazzeri went on record supporting the claims the pitches were no hoax – "I had no intention of striking out, I planned to hit the ball."

One sportswriter suggested after the game that, perhaps, "Mitchell's curves were too much for Ruth and Gehrig."

Another writer, in the April 4th, 1931 issue of the New York Times, claimed the pitches were no more than "mere gallantry" but did mention to compliment Mitchell, stating, "there are no such sluggers [like Ruth and Gehrig] in the Southern Association, and she may win laurels this season … the prospect grows gloomier for [those who believe women are too weak to play the game]."

The world will never know what Mitchell could have accomplished had she been allowed to continue playing.

After the game, she joined Kid Elberfeld's travelling semi-professional team, the Lookout Juniors. Later she appeared as a member of an occult-based ball club called The House of David, and also performing circus-type acts like pitching an entire game while sitting on the back of a donkey. But, at age 23, Mitchell's interest in side-show, shock-value baseball waned, so she gave up baseball to work at an office job for her father's company. A decade later, when the All-American Girl's Professional Baseball League asked her to join their debut season, she said no. She returned to professional baseball only once, in 1982, to throw out the ceremonial first pitch at Engel Stadium to kick off yet another season of Chattanooga Lookouts baseball more than 50 years after her historic feat on that same field.

From 1985 to her death in 1987, former general manager Bill Lee gave Mitchell free admission to Lookouts games.

"She simply had to call the office and I'd send my secretary to pick her up," Lee said. "She'd go to Jackie's house, pack up her beer and cigarettes and drive her to the games. She was a lot of fun and good to be around."

To this day, Mitchell is not a member of the National Baseball Hall of Fame, though Commissioner Landis has been a member since his death in 1944 and has the distinction of having the Most Valuable Player Award named in his honor. Mitchell's mentor, Dazzy Vance, was inducted in 1955, and Ruth – the man she struck out in four pitches – was a charter member at the Hall of Fame's creation in 1936. Even Gehrig, who retired from baseball July 4th, 1939 when he announced his diagnosis with the disease now bearing his name – Amyotrophic lateral sclerosis, or more commonly called "Lou Gehrig's Disease" – was inducted into the halls of Cooperstown.

Despite the critiques and the lack of a bronze plaque or the conspicuous absence of medals in her honor, no one or no thing – including time – can diminish Mitchell's accomplishment. Indeed, the day a seemingly unassuming teenage girl turned the tables on two legends of America's favorite pastime will not go down solely as a historic day in the life of the Chattanooga Lookouts, but as an unforgettable, undeniable triumph in the history of an American tradition.

Chapter Eight

The Voice of the Lookouts

Demanding of his players and the umpires, it stands to reason Joe Engel would demand a lot of his staff. And when Arch McDonald came to town, the Lookouts' first radio broadcaster learned just exactly how demanding Chattanooga's only millionaire could truly be.

Engel knew the team needed a voice to reach the city – a calm, resonant voice to broadcast the games into offices and factories throughout Chattanooga.

He found his answer in the throat of a 31-year-old Arkansas native, who wound up spending part of his school years in Chattanooga, where he played football at McCallie School.

Arch McDonald, a tall, full-framed young man with sandy brown hair, sharp features and a pleasant smile, spent a few years after high school graduation searching for his future in a variety of careers.

For more than a decade, McDonald crisscrossed the countryside working in the oil fields of Texas and the wheat fields of the Dakotas. For a time, he was a towel handler for legendary boxing great Jack Dempsey, which was possibly the place McDonald was first bit by sports broadcasting. In California, he pursued his luck as a Hollywood movie extra and later tried his hand at selling patent medicines.

When the stock market crashed and jobs ran scarce, McDonald returned home to Chattanooga, taking a low-profile job selling refrigerators. To satisfy his acquired taste for celebrity, McDonald took a job with a local radio station, WDOD, playing country records part-time.

In the months leading up to the 1932 season, Engel contacted the radio station about the possibility of broadcasting ball games. By opening day, the 31-year-old McDonald sat behind a microphone in the press box at the top of Engel Stadium.

His first year as the voice of the Lookouts, the team won the Southern League pennant and McDonald was recognized by "The Sporting News" as the nation's favorite broadcaster.

The magazine stated McDonald's, "clear, resonant voice and knowledge of sports has made his name a household word in the South."

Some speculate McDonald won the title because Engel – the notoriously eccentric promoter – stuffed the ballot box to drum up a little more media attention for his ball team.

With Engel, anything was possible.

It's true McDonald would do almost anything for Engel. When Engel brought the circus to the ballpark for a game, Arch called the play-by-play while riding on a camel's back. He later called the moment, "my crowning glory of radio."

So, is it feasible to think Engel would do anything he could to draw attention to his team? Of course!

Regardless of how McDonald won the title as the

Arch McDonald nicknamed Joe DiMaggio, "The Yankee Clipper."

most popular announcer, he took no time in proving himself worthy.

McDonald spent another season calling Lookouts games, coining many phrases still used from the big leagues to the little leagues.

For example, McDonald's broadcast might have sounded something like this:

"Chattanooga has two ducks on the pond with a man at the plate. Here comes the pitch and it's right down Broadway! A hard swing and there she goes, Mrs. Murphy! The Lookouts have really cut down the old pine tree!"

Now, the translation.

"Two ducks on the pond" meant there were two runners on base. Consequently, a double play would cause "two dead ducks." A pitch "right down Broadway" cut the center of the plate and McDonald exclaimed, "There she goes, Mrs. Murphy" whenever the Lookouts smacked a homerun.

Then there was the phrase, "They cut down the old pine tree," which stemmed from McDonald's experience turning country records on the radio and Engel's love of country music.

McDonald pulled the phrase from the title of a popular country song published in 1929, featured regularly on the Lum and Abner radio show. The song lyrics were surprisingly somber, lamenting the death of a young lover.

> *They cut down the old pine tree,*
> *And they hauled it away to the mill,*
> *To make a coffin of pine*
> *For that sweetheart of mine.*
> *They cut down the old pine tree.*
> *But she's not alone in her grave tonight,*
> *For it's there my heart will always be.*
> *Though we'd drifted apart,*
> *Still they cut down my heart*
> *When they cut down the old pine tree.*

Taken out of context, the song is depressing and ill-appropriate to suit the carefree mood of a Minor League Baseball game.

But McDonald touted the phrase after many of the Lookouts' successes on the field that thwarted any of the opposing teams' attempt to take control of the scoreboard.

In context, every time the Lookouts "cut down the old pine tree" by throwing a double play, striking out a batter, or hitting a homerun, they sent the opposing teams' hope for victory to an early grave in that pine coffin. McDonald went as far as to play the song over the PA system, making it a fan favorite, according to former player Hillis Layne.

"They'd play it in the seventh-inning and the crowd would sing along," Layne told Chattanoogan reporter Harmon Jolley in 2004. "That would really get the players going."

In 1934, McDonald got the call that would define his life's work.

After taking his club all the way to the World Series in 1933, Griffith realized he'd attracted a fresh set of fans. He decided it was time the Senators reached out to the crowds beyond the main gate by broadcasting games on the radio.

When Engel got the call from Griffith asking for advice, he knew just the man who could help introduce the Senators to the nation.

Arch McDonald left the city he'd called home for a second time, heading for the nation's capital.

When he arrived in Washington, D.C., he called the games for five years on two separate stations. He took his unique phrases, and his favorite country song, with him, making them part of Senators' club history.

In 1939, the New York Yankees – the Bronx Bombers – came calling for McDonald, asking him to come call the games in the House that Ruth Built. It was an offer the 38-year-old couldn't refuse.

Broadcasting alongside Mel Allen, he was the first to call Joe DiMaggio by his now famous nickname as the "Yankee Clipper."

73

But the Southern boy was not accustomed to the fast pace in the Big Apple, realizing he preferred Broadway to be only as close as the next strike down the center of home plate.

The start of the 1940 season found McDonald back in Washington with a renewed zeal. He spent the next 17 years calling games for the Senators, even re-enacting away games over the radio directed by Western Union telegraphs he received at the local drug store. After a short time, crowds would pack the drug store just to watch McDonald do the long-distance play-by-play.

In 1956, his career calling Senators games came to a close after the club changed advertisers. A few years later, the entire franchise was sold and moved to Minnesota, where they were renamed the Twins.

McDonald continued calling football games for the Washington Redskins, until his sudden death at age 59, on a train returning from a match with the New York Giants. McDonald was posthumously honored in 1999 with the Ford C. Frick Award, honoring journalists and broadcasters who made a considerable contribution to the game of baseball. He is featured with other award winners, like Chicago Cubs' great Harry Caray, in the "Scribes and Mikemen" exhibit in the Library of the National Baseball Hall of Fame in Cooperstown, New York.

Chapter Nine

A Slugging Legend and the Champs

At the same time Arch McDonald was taking the reigns in the press box high above Engel Stadium, Cecil Travis helped the Chattanooga Lookouts claim their first Southern Association championship.

Born the youngest of ten and raised on a Georgia cattle farm just south of Atlanta, Travis always had his eye on playing baseball in the big leagues. When he was a teenager, he attended an Atlanta baseball camp run by Kid Elberfeld.

Elberfeld knew Engel from his playing days, so he placed a call to Chattanooga after watching the 16-year-old farm-boy swing a bat. He told Engel that the Lookouts needed this kid on the team, claiming big things would come for the club if Travis were on the roster.

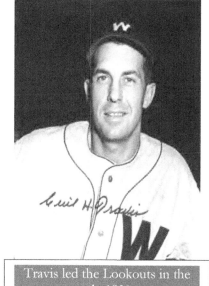

Travis led the Lookouts in the early 1930s.

Engel's scouting instincts prevailed and, in 1931, he signed the teenager to a contract.

Travis made his minor league debut hitting .429 in 13 games in 1931. The following season, as McDonald called the plays and the team pursued their first pennant since 1909, Travis hit .356 in 203 hits, claiming 88 RBIs, and he led the league in triples –

smacking an impressive 17 – and led the Lookouts in batting average.

Travis was just part of a stronger team led by Lookouts manager, Bert Niehoff, who came to Chattanooga to win baseball games, having claimed the league pennant twice before with Mobile and Atlanta.

All season, Chattanooga traded spots with Memphis back and forth leading the Southern Association in first place. By the season's end, Memphis finished ahead of the Lookouts by only a few games.

Engel was certain that his team could take the lead away from Memphis if they were allowed to play three games against Knoxville rained out during the regular season.

Off the field, Engel was suffering great tragedy and indulging in great joys. While he met his future bride, Hallie Birkhead at a Washington, D.C. party, he also mourned the loss of his only son, Joe Bryant – just nine years old – when the boy was struck by a car and killed.

Despite his personal life, he remained focused for the sake of the team.

He took his petition to the Association president, requesting Chattanooga be allowed to play the scrubbed games despite the season having officially ended. President Martin agreed with Engel, deeming the games could be played.

Fearful of losing the championship title, Memphis team manager Mr. Watkins appealed the issue to the Association's board of directors. After a vote, the board decided 5-3 the games could not be played.

Chattanooga's hopes for their first Association pennant were dashed – for the moment.

An adamant Engel took the matter straight to the commissioner of professional baseball, Judge Landis.

By appealing his case to the highest authority in the game, Engel received his verdict shortly after noon on September 9th.

The cancelled games would be played.

A relaxed Knoxville team, already having dispersed for the winter after finishing last in the league, quickly regrouped and traveled to Chattanooga for the first game in a best of three series. Chattanooga won 12-4 in six innings, when the umpires called the game on account of darkness.

The next two games were played in Knoxville, with Chattanooga winning both.

Association officials quickly tallied the scores and Chattanooga earned the Southern Association pennant, edging Memphis with a better overall winning percentage - .658 to .656. While a Memphis pitcher claimed the most wins in the Association that season, Lookouts pitcher Clyde Barfoot boasted the Association's lowest ERA – 2.76 through 254 innings of play.

Barfoot, Travis, and the championship Lookouts headed to Atlanta to play in the thirteenth consecutive year of the Dixie Series Championships. In their first appearance in the series, the Lookouts defeated the Texas League Champion Beaumont, Texas club, four games to one.

Impressed by Travis' play and the Lookouts' dual championships, Clark Griffith eagerly pulled the third baseman to the majors at the start of the 1933 season.

When an injury forced third baseman Ossie Bluege to sit out a few games, the 19-year-old Travis made the trip to Washington, D.C., to fill in.

On May 16, 1933, Travis stepped into the history books.

In a game against the Cleveland Indians, Travis stepped to the plate five times – hitting safely each time. Only one other player in the history of the game hit five times at five at-bats in his first game; a player named Fred Clarke in June 1894.

The Senators won the game 11 to 10 in twelve innings.

"My first game was a big thrill," an 89-year-old Travis told "Baseball Digests'" Todd Newville in 2003. "We beat them but there was a lot of hitting on both sides in that ballgame. I don't remember it going 12 innings, but I sure remember it was a big score."

Travis played a total of 18 games in Washington, carrying a .302 average, before Bluege was released from the injured list and returned to the field.

The remainder of the 1933 season saw Travis back in Chattanooga, after a firm clap on the back and a "Good job, rookie" from his Senator teammates.

Back under the watchful eye of Engel and in the safety of McDonald's vocals, Travis played with the hunger of a player who had tasted the sweet honey of the majors and wanted desperately to get back.

As a Lookout, he pounded another 185 hits, earned 74 RBIs, and drove his batting average up to .352.

By the beginning of the 1934 season, when the Lookouts started their five-year slide into seventh place, Griffith found a permanent place for Travis with the Senators.

He played in the majors for twelve more seasons over the next fifteen years, swatting .314 for his career and playing on the all-star team three times.

In 1941, Travis took second place in the American League to Ted Williams as top slugger, batting .359 and amassing 218 hits – a record he held until New York Yankee, Derek Jeter broke it in 1999.

The next season, Travis got his country's call to fight the Germans in World War II. He was away from baseball for three years, earning the rank of sergeant and suffering frozen feet in the Battle of the Bulge.

When he returned stateside in 1945, he played only two more seasons batting barely above .200 and getting only a handful of hits. As he bowed out of the game in 1947, he said, "I saw I wasn't helping the ball club, so I just gave it up."

Despite his quiet exit from the game, Travis made a big splash into professional baseball in Chattanooga, leading the club to a pennant win and its first Dixie Series title. He would be one of many Lookouts to leave an impact on the national pastime.

The 1932 club won the Lookouts first Southern League championship since 1892.

Chapter Ten

House Hunting

With just two league championships under the clubs' belt since 1909, Joe Engel knew he couldn't rely on winning seasons to attract a crowd to the ballpark.

So, in the 1930s, he earned a few nicknames – "Barnum of the Bush (Leagues)" for the circus-like atmosphere he portrayed at the stadium and the "Baron of Baloney," because of some of his more zany antics at the park. He quickly established himself as a renowned promoter.

Two of his greatest stunts came in the late 1930s.

In late winter of 1935, the publisher of the fledgling Chattanooga Times, Everett Allen, got an idea to promote his newspaper. He would build a house on a piece of property he owned, then give it away!

Following on the heels of a national recession, Allen knew people would come from miles around leaping at the opportunity to win a house. Most struggled to buy food and clothing. To win shelter would be a dream come true.

The publisher went to work, bartering with local contractors and builders to donate labor and supplies in exchange for advertising. Most responded eagerly and, within months, the house was constructed at 1 Rivermont Road, at the intersection of Hixson Pike, where it still stands today.

Retailers throughout the city were also eager to get involved. Many sold raffle tickets to their patrons. Every half-dollar of merchandise purchased at any participating retailer earned the customer a raffle ticket – one more chance to win the house! Since so many retailers decided to help distribute the tickets, Allen knew he would need a large venue to hold most of Chattanooga the day of the drawing.

Never one to miss an opportunity to draw a crowd, Joe Engel stepped in. The two men agreed to announce the winner of the house after the fifth inning of the Lookouts game in Engel Stadium May 2nd.

Neither man could have known the massive crowd that would descend on Engel Stadium on that May day.

By the time the artificial lights blinked on at the ballpark that fateful night, 26,639 men and women turned out to anxiously await the fifth inning announcement.

Fans line the outfield in May 1936.

The stadium, filled to capacity at 10,000 people, overflowed with fans. Engel roped off sections of the outfield against the wall, allowing fans to spill onto the playing field for a place to sit. Then he hurried to the dugout and put all the baseballs to be used in the game into the freezer. Frozen baseballs, he knew, wouldn't fly near as far as a regular baseball and he wasn't taking any chances of a fan getting hit by a pitch knocked deep into the outfield.

As the Lookouts left the field at the end of the fifth inning, 26,639 hearts started to pound; 53,278 hands fluttered for their stash of raffle tickets; and 53,278 eyes searched the field for any sign that might hint they were the proud owners of a new house.

Joe Engel walked onto the field, followed by a large brass wheel on the back of a flatbed truck stuffed with four million ticket stubs. Behind Engel was a young, African-American boy dressed in a yellow sun suit and rubber cap. The boy was blindfolded and lifted into the wheel. Engel rolled the wheel around a handful of times and then the boy fished out a ticket stub. The owner of the matching ticket won a brand new Lincoln Zephyr.

Next came the raffle for the house.

Again, the boy tumbled in the wheel and drew out a stub. The winning number was called.

No one moved.

For fifteen minutes, the stadium waited for the owner of the matching ticket to step forward.

No one did.

Later, a mother told newspaper reporters she was sure she had the matching ticket but blamed her son for losing it earlier in the week.

Without a winner, the wheel rolled again on the back of that flatbed truck and the boy fished out yet another ticket stub. Engel read the winning number and the crowd frantically shuffled papers, eager to see if the fates had awarded them a second chance to win the coveted prize.

Up in the stands along the first base line, a 26-year-old man named Charlie Mills sat by his friend and looked at his raffle tickets.

Mills, an employee working at the shipping and receiving department at H.G. Hills, then at the corner of Broad and Main streets, held the winning number.

"It didn't take me long to identify the winning ticket number," Mills told the Chattanooga Free Press the next day. "I flung the other tickets away, ploughed over my buddy who was next to me, but it seemed to me many, many minutes before I was able to make my way from my seat to the side of the big truck which carried the barrel."

The Lakeview, Georgia boy took no time getting to the field, according to Engel.

"He told me later that he did not know what was happening," Engel told the newspaper. "He said he thought he'd never get to the ticket wheel, his legs were so wobbly."

Engel congratulated the boy, saying he'd won a fine new house for his wife and family. When Mills replied that he wasn't married, Engel laughingly replied, "Son, you'll have ten thousand girls waiting just outside and you can pick your bride."

The game set a Southern Association attendance record and played a large role in cementing Engel's title as one of the best promoters in the history of the game.

But once is never enough.

On opening day in 1938, Joe Engel took Chattanooga on a wild elephant hunt. Actually, he brought a wild elephant hunt to Chattanooga.

The Baron of Baloney, having already brought the circus to the stadium like Barnum and Bailey would bring the big top to town, decided Chattanoogans would turn out in droves to see something as exotic as an elephant hunt on his baseball field!

So he spread the word far and wide that fans would see a wild elephant hunt at Engel Stadium on opening day.

When the fated spring day arrived, attendees took to their seats through side entrances to the park, unable to enter through the main concourse. Beneath their feet, under the bleachers in the concourse of the stadium, they heard heavy stomps and loud, fierce roars everyone was certain could only be made by massive, restless elephants anxiously awaiting their demise on the nearby field.

Excitement and anticipation rose as the crowds gathered in their seats and the noise from below grew more intense. When time came for the hunt to begin, the crowd turned their eyes to the field as the surging mammoths fled from beneath the stands.

"In the elephant hunt, fourteen colored lads, dressed only in white shorts and carrying long spears, danced to three tom-toms," wrote Wirt Gammon in a 1938 article for the Chattanooga Times. "After six hunters, wearing bamboo hats, carrying automatic shotguns and riding wooden hobby horses appeared, the 'cannibals' rounded up the herd of elephants – made of cloth – and then began the bombardment. Almost 50 shots were fired before an elephant was bagged and only two were 'killed' during the chase."

Nearly twenty men donning a dozen cloth elephant suits awkwardly tromped onto the field as Joe Engel leveled the barrel of his rifle, loaded with blanks, at the costume pachyderms.

"Walk Softly, and Carry a Laminated Wooden Stick". Joe Engel owned his own bat manufacturing company – the Joe Engel Bat Company – which produced the first laminated wooden bats sold nationally.

The crowd roared with laughter as the elephants toppled over with each shot. Many fans were certain they came to see an actual elephant hunt at the corner of O'Neal and East Third Street. The act did so well, Engel took it on the road, performing the wild elephant hunt at other Association ballparks for the next few years.

Engel's apparent blindness to racial sensitivity transcended beyond the elephant hunt.

When he acquired a Native American pitcher, he used the player to re-enact a skit he called "Custer's Revenge."

The pitcher, Chief Woody Arkeketa, would follow Engel onto the field from the dugout as the latter lured the player with a jug marked 'FIREWATER' to the tune of "Beer Barrel Polka." Engel wound his way toward the infield to a teepee set up on the mound. Once the pitcher and Engel were inside, five separate explosions would rock the tent along with blood-curdling screams. In a matter of moments, Arkeketa – donning a bald wig – would run from the teepee with a man, dressed to look like General Custer, in hot pursuit with a butcher knife in one hand and a wig of long hair in the other.

On yet another occasion, Engel acquired a pitcher of Chinese ancestry, George Hoy, though the boy spent his entire life in Brooklyn. At the start of a double header, in which Hoy was scheduled to pitch, Engel announced tongue-in-cheek, "Hoy can't play this one. He's upstairs doing my laundry. But he'll play in the second game."

Chapter Eleven

"Wanna Buy a Ball Club?"

By the end of the 1936 season, Engel set Association attendance records, brought a league championship home to Chattanooga, and harvested a few major league greats – both on the field and in the broadcast booth.

While major league clubs continued to flounder through the mid-1930s, Engel prospered. In 1935, Clark Griffith sold his best player, Joe Cronin to the Boston Red Sox. The Senators struggled to win games and draw crowds so Griffith turned his attention to his farm system.

On January 17th, 1937, Griffith sent his adopted son, Calvin, to Chattanooga. Calvin came with specific orders. He would replace Engel as the president of the Lookouts.

Desperate to restore his major league ball club to its glory days during the club's decade of victory from the late 1920s to mid 1930s, Griffith put his faith in Engel to build a strong foundation for his organization.

The moment Engel stepped down as the Lookouts' president, he accepted a position as the general manager of the Washington Senators farm system. At the time, that included Chattanooga; Trenton, New Jersey; and Sanford, Florida.

Chattanooga saw and heard immediate reaction to the change. News reporters listed their objections to dethroning Engel and voiced their concern for the prosperity of the club under Calvin. The only consolation to those mourning the loss of Engel was his decision to stay in Chattanooga, making his namesake stadium his base of operations.

That season in the nation's capital wasn't a good one and, by mid-season, Griffith made the decision to sell the Lookouts and use the money to patch holes in the Senators shaky financial foundation.

His asking price? $125,000.

The self-proclaimed king of baseball leapt into action on July 16th, determined not to see baseball leave Chattanooga while under someone else's care.

Engel's salary was approximately one-fifth Griffith's asking price. He knew he couldn't purchase the team on his own; he'd need some help.

Engel took his problem to the people of Chattanooga, selling shares of ownership in the ball team for five dollars each.

> **"The Wrong Place at the Wrong Time"**
>
> When umpire Buck Campbell came to a game in Chattanooga after learning the Knoxville-Nashville game he was scheduled to work was postponed, Joe Engel decided to have some fun. After each half-inning of Lookouts play, Engel had the scoreboard operator post half-inning results from Knoxville as if the game were actually underway! Campbell shot to the phone in a panic, afraid he was an hour south of the game he was supposed to officiating. When he returned to his seat after learning the truth, Engel was beside himself with laughter.

Newspaper accounts stated it was not uncommon to find Joe Engel standing on a street corner, asking passersby, "Wanna buy a ball club?"

By September 5th, Joe Engel and 1,532 Chattanoogans bought the Lookouts from Clark Griffith and the Senators.

Nine corporate investors pledged $35,000 while the public purchased 4,095 shares for a total of $20,475. Engel pledged the remaining $47,000 and Griffith – pleased to see his old friend would own the club – dropped his asking price to $100,000.

The change in ownership brought with it a change in management. Engel reinstated his authority as president of the club, while the dethroned Calvin left Chattanooga to manage a smaller club in Charlotte, North Carolina.

Sportswriters hailed the move, welcoming Engel back to his rightful spot as ruler of the roost at the stadium bearing his name.

The season apart seemed to only strengthen Engel's bond with his club and their love for him.

In 1938 and 1939, Engel brought two baseball legends to Chattanooga and laid the groundwork for yet another championship team.

Midway through the 1938 season, Rogers Hornsby – The Rajah – came to town.

Hornsby was, without argument, one of the greatest hitters of all time. He was the National League batting champion for seven seasons in the 1920s, played in two World Series, batted a career average . 358 – a National League record – and slugged a 20th century record high .424 in 1924. Hornsby topped the .400 mark  three times and was the first National League player to hit more than 300 homeruns.

Sportswriter Joe Williams once said of Hornsby, "If consistency is a jewel, then Mr. Hornsby is a whole rope of pearls."

During one game, a rookie pitcher disputed Hornsby's count of three balls and no strikes. The umpire replied, "Young man, when you throw a strike, Mr. Hornsby will let you know."

However, The Rajah's legend was not in his bat, but in his mouth. As a playing manager, Hornsby was bounced from team to team, despite his incomparable athletic abilities.

The Rajah was notorious for constantly openly belittling his teammates and team owners, showing little respect for anyone who held a different opinion than his own or failed to perform as well as he could.

In the fall of 1926, as Hornsby led his team to a World Series championship as a playing manager, the team owner scheduled an exhibition game in New Haven, Connecticut.

Rogers spoke out publicly, saying the owner – his boss – was "a money-grubbing cheapskate" who didn't have the team's best interest at heart. Hornsby stated his players needed the day to rest as they played in the post-season. By Christmas, Hornsby was traded to the New York Giants.

He only stayed in New York for a single season before heading to Boston, after he told a newspaper reporter the club could never win the pennant as long as Eddie Ferrel was playing shortstop. Ferrel was dining out with Hornsby at the time of the interview.

The Red Sox gave Hornsby his walking papers after a single season as well. They should have known better. Upon starting in May, Hornsby answered the question, "Can this team win a pennant?" saying, "Not with these humpty-dumpties."

In September 1930, he became the manager of the Chicago Cubs, where he stayed until mid-season 1932. The Cubs traded five players plus $200,000 to acquire Hornsby, who made their risk worth while when he led the Cubs to a pennant win by 10 ½ games.

Then, The Rajah made a decision during late innings of a tied ballgame with the Atlanta Braves that would end his stint in the Windy City.

Hornsby pulled hitter, Rollie Hemsley, and decided to pinch-hit in Hemsley's place. The phenomenal hitter won the game for the Cubs, socking a grand-slam homerun, but lost the respect of all his players. When the clubs' owner asked Hornsby what he was thinking, Rogers confidently replied, "I know I'm a better hitter than Hemsley." When the team won the World Series at the end of 1932, under the leadership of a new manager, they voted to cut Hornsby out of sharing in the winnings.

The first half of the 1938 season, Hornsby worked as the batting coach of the Milwaukee Brewers – a minor league team for the Boston Red Sox. While there, he mentored Ted Williams, of whom he said "he's not a great hitter," because Williams couldn't hit to left field when outfielders shifted to the right.

Later that year, Hornsby came to Chattanooga where he finished out the season managing the Lookouts. At his first trip to the plate, pinch-hitting as a Lookout, he hit one of his legendary homeruns over the leftfield wall.

While it's not clear what made Hornsby's trip to the Scenic City of the South so brief, history offers a laundry list of reasons why his managing career didn't last.

In 1942, he was inducted into the Hall of Fame.

He later worked as a scout for the New York Mets, becoming a master of blunt honesty when commenting on prospects, with reports reading "too fat", "glasses", or "he didn't impress me."

In Ken Burns' popular documentary, Baseball, historians stated Hornsby's faults as a manager stemmed from his overwhelming successes as a player.

"[His player's] failure to match his own intensity kept him in an almost perpetual rage."

While undergoing surgery in Chicago to remove cataracts in 1963, a minor heart attack and a blood clot claimed Hornsby's life at age 64.

Chattanooga is truly lucky that, though it seems like the blink of an eye, His Excellency of the National League graced the playing field at the corner of East Third and O'Neal.

The next season, in 1939, Hazen Shirley "Kiki" Cuyler, replaced Hornsby as the captain of the club.

Managing in Chattanooga was like coming home for Cuyler, who got his start playing Minor League Baseball at Sulpher Dell for the Vols in Nashville, Tennessee.

He earned his nickname in Nashville, where players would call his name when a fly ball came his way in centerfield. The second baseman and the shortstop would yell, "Cuy! Cuy!" and the sportswriter at the park deemed him "Kiki" in 1923.

Kiki went to the majors in 1924 and was named to the all-star team in 1925. In 1926 and 1928 through 1930, the left-fielder led the National League in stolen bases. He totaled 2,299 hits during his career with a lifetime batting average of .321, spending most of his playing days with the Pittsburgh Pirates and Chicago Cubs.

While with the Pirates, Cuyler went head-to-head against Clark Griffith and the Washington Senators in the 1925 World Series, in which he drove in the winning run off a pitch from Walter Johnson.

Four years later, while with the Cubs, Cuyler would pound an impressive .360 and help the Cubs best his former Pittsburgh teammates to win the World Series.

When he was released by the Brooklyn Dodgers at the end of the 1938 season, Kiki came to Chattanooga where he started a ten-year stretch managing in the Southern Association.

> **"Go Jump in a River"**
> During World War II, Engel brought a displaced German family to America to live on his horse farm until the war ended. He also spent a lot of time promoting USO drives, selling war bonds on the radio.
> When one man called and said, "I'll buy a $50,000 bond, if you get off the air," Engel replied, "If you buy a $50,000 bond, I'll do better than that. I'll jump into the Tennessee River."
> Though it was wintertime, Engel was prepared to follow through with his word, but the Coast Guard stopped his dutiful leap.

As a semi-regular player, Cuyler brought his winning ways to the field, leading the Lookouts to win the league pennant in 1939.

Kiki's first year managing at Chattanooga was an eventful one.

Four teams that season raced neck-and-neck to claim the Southern Association title – Chattanooga, Memphis, Nashville, and Atlanta – with Knoxville nipping at the heels of the pack.

In July, Engel sold the team's best slugger – Bill Nicholson, who carried a .334 average for the season – to the Chicago Cubs for $35,000. In his place, the Lookouts picked up a rookie from the Single A Senators farm club in Spartanburg, South Carolina, by the name of Allen McElreath.

Cuyler made a public announcement that the Lookouts weren't planning to win a championship. Rather, they'd spend the rest of the season building for next year.

With a few weeks left in the season, Memphis again led the Association in the race for the pennant, just as they had in 1932. Except this time, Memphis held a nine-game lead over second place Nashville. The Lookouts held a close third when the Nashville Vols pulled ahead of Memphis to claim first place in early September.

But with the pennant race so close by the season's end, Cuyler saw his chance to strike on September 8th and took it. Memphis and Nashville both lost doubleheaders, putting Chattanooga in first place.

> "Full Service"
> In 1940, Joe Engel hired local radio legend, Luther Masingill, while the young boy was working at a gas station. As the owner of the WDEF radio station, Engel asked Luther to be the telephone receptionist but, after hearing his clear, deep voice, he had Masingill record a demo tape. On New Year's Eve, Masingill made his radio broadcast debut where he spent the rest of his illustrious career.

With Memphis slated to play Nashville, Chattanooga only had to defeat New Orleans to keep a grip on the title.

Cuyler put his players' noses to the grindstone, pushing four batters who had hit consistently in the high .200s all season – Stan Benjamin, Babe Barnum, Ralph McAdams, and Alex Hooks – to boost their averages above .300.

Cuyler

The Lookouts defeated the Pelicans 6-2 when the rookie McElreath stole home and pitcher Dick Lanahan threw his nineteenth victory of the season and posted a season ERA of 2.95.

The crowd of 10,624 were stunned and ecstatic, certain only a few months earlier the club would have no chance for the title. Chattanooga won just 85 of 150 games, as opposed to their 1932 win record of 98 of 149 games.

Still, the Lookouts claimed the pennant over second place Memphis by just a game and a half and eleven percentage points - .567 to Memphis' .556.

Nashville finished twelve points behind the Lookouts with an overall win percentage of .555. Atlanta settled into fourth with .553 and Knoxville finished fifth of the eight-team Association with .520.

The next season – his last as a playing manager – Cuyler got a hit at his only at-bat, then was relegated to the bench managing in 1941, the year the Association abolished the playing-manager.

Opportunity came calling in 1942 when the Lookouts' largest rival, the Atlanta Crackers, offered him a managing job. Kiki stayed in Atlanta until 1949, when he was called back to the majors to serve as the head coach of the Boston Red Sox.

In February 1950, Cuyler died ten days after suffering a heart attack while ice fishing near his home in Michigan at the young age of 52. He was inducted into the Hall of Fame in 1968.

As for the Lookouts, the best was yet to come.

In 1941, the Senators reclaimed ownership of the locally-owned Lookouts, despite an injunction filed in U.S. District Court by two local stock holders to keep ownership of the Lookouts local.

Additionally, on the heels of the club's fourth overall pennant win, Chattanooga would come to host one of the greatest Minor League Baseball players ever to play the game.

Chapter Twelve

"One of the Best"

Hillis Layne slides safely into the base for this photo taken during his playing years in Chattanooga.

Ivoria Hillis "Hilly" Layne, one of the top minor league players of all time, was born in Whitwell, a rural town in Marion County, in Southeast Tennessee on February 4, 1919 – ten years before Joe Engel came to town.

By the time he was a teenager, Layne was infatuated with baseball. Living only twenty minutes away from Chattanooga, he constantly heard of Engel's exploits and the Lookouts.

He was 11 when the Senators bought the franchise and built Engel Stadium. At 12, he heard of the legendary Babe Ruth and Lou Gehrig striking out to the female pitcher for the hometown team.

"I dreamed of playing baseball in Engel Stadium," Layne told me, now 87-years old and still recovering from a 16-foot fall from a ladder in 1990. "I told my mother someday I would play in

Yankee Stadium and I was going to hit a homerun. Babe Ruth was my idol; I still say he was the greatest."

In 1932, at age 13, the Whitwell boy started playing ball for the local semipro team, which was part of the Sequatchie Valley Baseball League.

Though he started out playing against teams from surrounding cities, such as Jasper and South Pittsburg, Tennessee, Layne's eyes were always set on more lofty ambitions: Minor League Baseball in Chattanooga, then Major League Baseball including a trip to the "House that Ruth built" in New York City.

The teenager from rural Tennessee knew he had a long row to hoe in order to see such dreams come true.

For five years he played baseball, went to school, and met a girl – Dorothy Jean, five years his junior. Between schoolwork and ball games, she and Layne courted. As their affection for each other grew, so did the Sequatchie Valley League, expanding to include teams in Bridgeport and Stevenson, Alabama – changing the league name to the Tennessee-Alabama League.

In 1937, Layne graduated from high school, was falling deeper in love with a girl named "Dottie" and was a rising star of the Whitwell ball club.

"I remember playing with tar and tape baseballs and, sometimes, I played with no glove in the outfield," Layne recalled.

One Sunday afternoon, the 18-year-old joined his teammates in the bed of a United Coal Mine truck for a trip to Chattanooga, where the team played a double header against the best team in the league – a group of wool-mill workers employed by Peerless Woolens.

"Everybody said they had the best pitchers in the [Tennessee-Alabama] League," Layne said.

While facing those pitchers on that fated Sunday afternoon, Layne's life would change forever.

He hit seven out of ten trips to the plate during that game, shaming the best pitchers in the league and claiming the title of most outstanding player by days' end. As he ambled to the truck, climbed into the back and waited for the return trip home, two well-dressed men slowly made their way toward him.

"We didn't have scouts back then like they have now," Layne said.

But he knew who the men were. Golf pros at area courses in Chattanooga – and confidantes of Lookouts owner, Joe Engel.

"They walked toward the truck and they were looking at me," he recalled. "I remember thinking what in the world do they want? So I climbed out of the truck to talk to them."

The men said they'd watched the game, saw Hillis play, and then asked a simple, straightforward question that would impact the rest of his life.

"Have you ever wanted to play baseball professionally?"

"Of course, I said yes," Layne said. "It's all I'd wanted to do. They told me to meet them at Engel Stadium at ten o'clock the next morning, and they said Joe Engel would be there."

Certainly, the budding athlete slept as restlessly as a child on Christmas Eve and, at 10 a.m. Monday, he stood with the two men from the day before and met one of the most outrageous promoters in the history of the game.

"They asked me again if I wanted to play and I said yes."

Engel gave the nod and then left, on his way to a game, while his secretary helped Layne fill out the appropriate paperwork to join the club.

The following spring, just months after his 19th birthday, Layne made his professional baseball debut, playing Class D ball in Americus, Georgia.

It was the start of an illustrious 19-year playing career for Layne – one wherein he would bat above .280 in eighteen of nineteen seasons, and never dip below .300 for fifteen. A career that saw his batting average lead his respective leagues on two occasions – once in Seattle and a second time in Lewiston, Idaho.

Defensively, he played out of the infield only one season, while the other nineteen seasons he spent at third base.

In his first two seasons, he played Class D ball in Americus, Georgia and Class C ball in Sanford, Florida, in the Washington Senators farm system. At second base for both teams, he played 156 games, scored 112 runs while driving in another 91 runners, stole five bases, hit six homeruns, 29 doubles, 15 triples and boasted a batting average of .310.

It took very little time for Joe Engel to recognize Layne's raw talent.

In 1940, Hillis started the season as a Chattanooga Lookout.

The most daunting aspect of

(From Left) Skeet McDaniels, Hillis Layne, and Johnny Sullivan try out for shortstop at spring training.

being a Lookout, according to Layne, wasn't the baseball legend and then-coach, Kiki Cuyler. It wasn't Joe Engel's "very aggressive, rah-rah" nature. The fact Engel was known for trading players who let their batting averages dip below .300 (incidentally, a mark enviable by most of today's major leaguers) was not the most intimidating part of playing at Engel Stadium.

It was that centerfield wall, which stretched for a record setting 471 feet at its deepest point.

"[The next season], I hit four homers inside the park. I hit down on the ball for line drives and had them roll up on the

Lookouts sign," Layne remembered. "It's a wonder anyone could hit a ball far enough to clear the wall."

While Cuyler worked the right field fence in batting practices, Layne concentrated his efforts on gaining more control of his hits, guiding the ball to the perfect holes so he could get on base safely.

His first season in Chattanooga, Layne scored 22 runs off 42 hits from 137 at-bats in 60 games. Despite an outstanding showing, batting .307 his first trip to Class AA ball, Layne ended the season in Selma, Alabama, where he played just six games.

However the move was only temporary because, in the spring of 1941, Joe Engel came calling on Layne a second time.

The Lookouts' shortstop, Skeet McDaniel, got into a fight in a Chattanooga hotel with an Indian chief. The scuffle left McDaniel with a broken arm and he was unable to play the rest of the season. Engel, still fresh with the memory of Layne's impressive showing the previous season, knew just the man to replace his injured shortstop.

However, the manager at Class C Selma, Alabama, in the Southeastern League, wasn't eager to lose such a promising and gifted player.

Selma's manager was angry about losing Layne before the season started. Most players at that time progressed through the farm system ranks gradually, spending a year at each level – Class D, Class C, Class B, Class A, Class AA, Class AAA, then on to the majors. Layne's strong bat and quick defense on the field drew attention in both Americus and Sanford. When Selma got Layne at the end of the 1940 season for only six games, the manager was certainly eager for the following year when Layne would benefit his team in their pursuit of top standings in the Southeastern League.

Now, in a blink, Engel was taking those dreams away.

"Those two men got into a real rhubarb," Layne said. "It ended with me on a bus headed for Chattanooga and Engel sending a truck full of ice to Selma. They unloaded the ice in the manager's office and Engel said he could use it to cool down. Engel was quite a prankster."

One can only hope it was a large truck. Layne never stepped foot in Selma again and 1941 was his best season yet.

The 22-year-old scored 86 times off 181 hits from 536 at-bats in 142 games. He doubled 30 times, tripled ten times, and hit a dozen homeruns in front of crowds ranging between 7,500 to 10,500. Additionally, he drove in 82 runners, stole seven bases, and was hitting .338 late in the season when he got the call from Washington.

It was early one Saturday morning when Engel gave Layne and two other players the news – the Old Fox had called them up to play a double header the next day against the Cleveland Indians in Griffith Stadium for the Washington Senators.

"I didn't have a car, so I rode with another player," Layne said. "We made it all the way to Roanoke by the time we stopped Saturday night."

It was in Roanoke, Virginia, that Layne heard Senators announcer, Arch McDonald, give the news over the radio that would make Layne's knees go weak. The Indians planned to start Bob Feller on the mound in the first game at 2 p.m. – a pitcher with a recorded 110-mile-per-hour fast ball.

"Bob Feller was the best pitcher of my time – I'd say of all time," Layne recalls. "Nolan Ryan [who played for the Houston Astros and Texas Rangers in the 1970s, '80s and 90s] threw around 97 miles per hour. Imagine a kid just up from the minors having to hit that on his first game in the majors."

Layne recalls he stood his ground that game and, when Feller sent 17 batters back to the dugout, he failed to strike out the ambitious boy from Whitwell.

Layne finished the season as a Washington Senator, scoring eight runs off 50 hits from 141 trips to the plate in 13 games. He doubled twice, stole one base and nabbed six RBIs, ending his brief first appearance in the majors with a .280 average.

Everything was going "Hilly" Layne's way.

Then, in 1942, everything changed.

Only a handful of months after Japanese kamikaze pilots sunk U.S. battleships and claimed thousands of lives in an attack on Pearl Harbor, Hillis Layne got a call from Uncle Sam. Within weeks, he went from being the promising new rookie at the nation's capital, to Private First Class I. Hillis Layne of the United States Air Corps.

The Chattanooga Lookouts lost many players, having to pull an entirely new roster from Class B ball. The media called the crew, "The Kids" and "Joe Engel's Kindergarten."

For Layne, things took a turn for the better when some of his superior officers informed him they intended for him to serve his tour of duty in Fort Oglethorpe, Georgia – a mere twenty minutes south of Chattanooga – where he would play baseball as a member of the Air Corps' semi-pro team.

"I called my parents around 11 p.m. and told them the news, that I'd be staying in Chattanooga," Layne said. "Then, at 3 a.m., my sergeant turned the lights on in our barracks and told everyone to pack up ... we were all being reassigned to Keesler Field [in Biloxi, Mississippi]. My paperwork to get assigned to the ball team never had time to process."

For the next two months, while baseball continued despite concerns from Commissioner Landis [President Roosevelt urged the game to go on so Americans could have an entertaining distraction from the war], Layne worked himself to exhaustion building an airfield in the Mississippi heat.

A suspicion that Layne might be developing typhus fever in his left leg was confirmed two months after his move to Biloxi. The leg turned black and he spent 13 weeks in the infirmary.

Whether Layne would walk again was of secondary concern. At the time, doctors feared for his life.

"I almost died," he remembered. "That leg swole up three inches larger than the other leg – I measured it several times."

Eventually the fever subsided, though it never completely left him, and Layne was released from his military obligations on disability discharge. For reasons still unknown to Layne, the military officially regarded his medical trauma as a pre-existing condition and denied him a pension.

In 1943, Layne was a two-legged former baseball player, two years removed from the sport, with only one good leg.

In his seemingly darkest hour, he faced his dawn – a reunion with his childhood sweetheart, Dorothy "Dottie" Jean.

At 25 years of age, in 1944, the mending Hillis married his 20-year-old bride, whom he'd remain with until her unexpected death to cancer 54 years later. The couple had two children – a son, Steve, and daughter, Beth – who would give the couple four grandchildren.

The add below featured Hillis Layne during his playing days in Seattle.

Layne doesn't dispute Dottie's role in inspiring him to continue pursuing his dreams. She was his biggest fan, and he was hers.

In the spring of 1944, Hillis Layne – bed-ridden not so long

ago and clinging to life – walked back onto the field at Griffith Stadium.

"It was like a miracle to go through what I did and still walk back through the doors of the major leagues."

His first year back was, without question, the most trying of his career. He batted a meager .195 in 33 games, hitting only 17 times in 87 at-bats.

But he kept pushing himself, determined to achieve his goal – to fulfill a promise he'd made to his mother more than a decade ago.

The next season, his dream was realized.

In his third season as a Major League Baseball player, Layne saw action in 61 games, stepping to the plate 147 times, scoring 23 runs off 44 hits and driving in 14 other runners. He doubled five times, tripled four times, and hit a rousing .299.

But the most important statistic – the run that made up one of the most significant moments in Layne's life – is represented by a single tally mark in the homerun column.

In 1945 – two years after he pulled himself out of bed with the use of only one leg, seven years after he first stepped onto a professional baseball field, and twelve years after he joined a semi-pro team in a rural corner of Southeast Tennessee – Hillis Layne hit a homerun in Yankee Stadium.

Just like he told Mama he would.

"I had a goal to play professional baseball and hit a homerun in Yankee Stadium," he told me, "and I fulfilled it."

Layne has one other memorable experience from his days playing against the New York Yankees. He once took a line drive to the stomach from Joe DiMaggio.

"All I saw was a little puff of dust, the ball hit right in front of me then bounced up and hit me in the naval," he said. "I caught the ball, tossed it to second and we threw the double play to end the inning. When we walked to the dugout, the guys told me not to rub it – that would let DiMaggio know he's got something. For about six weeks, I could see the stitches from the ball around my navel."

In 1946, he returned to Chattanooga as a Lookout, where he hit .369, scoring 117 runs off 205 hits from 556 at-bats in 146 games. He doubled 32 times, tripled a dozen, hit seven homers, and drove in 82 base runners.

Also that season, Layne hit safely for 51 of 52 games [close to the record of 56 held by DiMaggio, though Layne's were not consecutive].

"I hit for 27 games safely then, on a Saturday night, the Atlanta Crackers sent me 0 for 3. Then I did 24 more. I knew a little bit then what it must have been like for Joe DiMaggio. You've got to have good ball control to hit safely for that long in order to know where to put the ball then put it there."

Layne spent the next four seasons leading the Class AAA Seattle Raniers, where manager and baseball great Casey Stengel said Layne, "put the bat on the ball as good as Stan Musial."

"That was such a great compliment," Layne told me, through a broad smile.

He played for the Raniers as part of the Pacific Coast League before major league teams like the Los Angeles Dodgers and San Francisco Giants arrived in the west. The Pacific Coast teams – the Portland Beavers, Los Angeles Angels, and other teams in Hollywood, San Diego, and San Francisco – dominated the coastline.

The add above portrayed Layne – then a Seattle Rainier – as a powerhouse at the plate.

His first year on the west coast, Layne led the league, batting .367, scoring 84 runs with 183 hits from 499 at-bats in 138 games.

Of Layne, one Seattle announcer said, he "needs to take two strikes before he starts to hit," to which Layne replied, "I didn't like striking out. I fought against it."

Layne spent eight more seasons playing baseball out west, mostly as a playing manager – a position eventually removed from professional baseball. He played a half season in Portland, Oregon; one in San Antonio; two in Anderson, Texas; one in Pine Bluff, Arkansas; a single season in San Angelo, Texas; and his final four seasons in Lewiston, Idaho, where he again led the league with a batting average of .391.

His final eight seasons, he hit .302, .306, .385, .367, .391, .354, .340, and .362. When he left the game as a player, he was 39 years old.

For another 11 years, Layne worked as a scout with the likes of pitching legend Dizzy Dean – a former teammate from his days in Sanford, Florida.

When the nation turned 200, Layne bowed out of the national pastime, leaving behind a career that tied "Hilly" with some of baseball's legends – Ted Williams, Walter Johnson, Joe DiMaggio, Dizzy Dean, and Casey Stengel, to recap just a few.

In 1978, the Society for American Baseball Research named Layne one of the top Minor League Baseball players of all time. He left the game with a lifetime batting average of .358, playing more than 1,800 professional games.

Despite his 16-foot fall in 1990 while trimming a tree branch that shattered his spine and left him dependent on braces or a wheelchair to move around, Layne's spirit is still indomitable.

Today, in his Signal Mountain, Tennessee home, he lives for his grandchildren – two in college at Clemson; the other two, ages 4 and 6, living just down the hallway from Grand-daddy's bedroom.

"The other night [youngest grandchild] Jack came into my room and gave me a hug. I told him that, when he comes to give me a hug goodnight, it does my heart so much good," Layne told me, emotion tugging at his voice and filling his eyes. "He said he prays for me and I know he's added years to my life."

Layne also said he has a new goal, now that he has his homerun in Yankee Stadium.

"My goal now is spiritual," he said. "I want to go to heaven and I'm really working at it – maybe God will take me in."

There is little doubt what lies ahead for Layne, even after God calls him home.

The Creator of the Universe will almost surely meet him, saying, "Well done, my good and faithful servant. Oh, and Hilly? Good game."

Chapter Thirteen

Willie Mays and the Choo Choos

While Hillis Layne made a bus trip to Chattanooga from Selma, in exchange for three tons of ice, a new baseball team was budding in the Lookout City.

In 1940, Beck Shepherd, owner of East Ninth Shoe Shine Parlor, was rounding up players for his semi-pro "blackball" team, the Chattanooga Choo Choos. Though the club wasn't part of the newly reformed Negro American League, and lasted only six years, Shepherd was the first team owner to let the "Say Hey" Kid play ball on a professional field.

Born in Whitfield, Alabama, on May 6, 1931, William Howard Mays grew up a gifted athlete. At his high school in Fairfield, Alabama, he was the football team's quarterback and an all-state basketball player. But Mays harbored a love for baseball – a love his father fanned and his mother feared.

As a medal-winning sprinter herself, she knew the potential pain her son faced pinning his hopes and dreams on a life as an athlete in a world divided by color. Instead of baseball, she urged her son to focus on school but his father pushed him to exceed on the playing field. The pair divorced over the issue.

When she died at only 34 years of age, Willie's father was free to openly encourage his son's pursuit of his dreams.

He took Mays into Birmingham to watch games played by the Birmingham Black Barons of the Negro Southern League, and he spent top dollar on name-brand equipment – Featherweight metal spikes and quality gloves – demanding his son devote his attention to baseball.

"[My father] didn't want me to work at a job. He didn't want me taking all that time away from baseball," Mays said. "I think I had a job as a dishwasher in a diner, but not for very long. He wanted me playing ball, learning from the game."

Possibly out of respect for his late-wife's wishes, Mays' father kept him out of the game professionally until he completed high school.

Beck Shepherd (second from left) discovered young Willie Mays (center above and pictured at right) when he was just in high school. Though he wasn't paid, Mays made his professional baseball debut in Chattanooga.

But the fifteen-year-old outfielder for the Fairfield High School Gray Sox idolized Joe DiMaggio and yearned for the day he could join the ranks of professional baseball.

Little more than an hour northeast of Fairfield lay the answer to Mays' prayer for a life in the big leagues.

Playing at Lincoln Park and Engel Stadium, the Chattanooga Choo Choos – a semi-pro team of black baseball players – attracted Mays' attention. While they weren't a professional team affiliated with the Negro Southern League, they drew plenty of attention from nearby Southern Association teams since they played at Joe Engel's ballpark.

The Chattanooga Lookouts' Class AA ball club was the last stop for rising athletes bound for the majors, and Mays must have known this was his chance to draw some big league attention while he was still in high school.

So Willie and his father drove from Fairfield to Chattanooga many times during the summers of 1945 and 1946 – Mays' freshman and sophomore years in high school – so Mays could take to the field potentially playing in front of big league scouts in town to recruit the Lookouts.

He honored his mother's wishes not to play professional baseball before graduating high school, and he never signed a contract with the Choo Choos.

"Yes, I discovered Willie," Shepherd said years later. "I saw him go get some hard hit balls and saw him get rid of them. Even then, he was a natural ballplayer – a great ballplayer. I said to myself right then – get this boy on your Choo Choos and you've got it made. He's the best."

In 1996, Mays told a reporter for the Chattanooga Times Free Press that he remembered staying in The Martin Hotel during his trips to Chattanooga, on North Street – now located on Martin Luther King, Jr. Boulevard.

During the middle of the 1946 season, Beck Shepherd went broke and the Chattanooga Choo Choos folded – only in existence for a handful of years and failing to draw a large enough crowd to pay the bills.

With a payroll of $3,300 per month, Shepherd knew it would be expensive to maintain the team. He blamed the end of the club on a string of bad weather through the 1946 season that followed the team across the country, canceling games, preventing ticket sales, and losing business.

Shepherd lost $17,000 before going completely broke and disbanding the team.

After two years of semi-professional baseball, Mays returned home and focused on high school.

In 1948 he graduated and was promptly picked up by the nearby Birmingham Black Barons to play ball, where he stayed for two seasons. In 1950, his ticket came when the New York Giants signed the amazing outfielder to a contract – taking Mays from Birmingham, to Trenton, New Jersey and, finally, to Minneapolis, Minnesota.

"Nobody ever came up to me and say like you see in a book; This is the way to play centerfield. I used to wish someone would tell me just how you do everything," Mays said of his five-year stint in semi-pro and minor league ball. "But it doesn't bother me now because I have learned that nobody can teach you nothing like you can learn yourself. You got to learn for yourself and you got to do it your own way."

The Giants paid $10,000 for Mays – plus a $5,000 signing bonus – to win a bidding war against the Boston Braves.

When he joined the Giants in 1951, he was quickly frustrated with his inability to put his bat on a major league pitch. Mays even asked his manager, Leo Durocher, to bump him back to the minors until he could help the team at the plate.

But his fielding abilities were already beyond compare, as he was consistently seen shagging long fly balls in the outfield over his shoulder with his left hand while holding his ball cap in his right. Durocher put Mays at ease, saying, "you're my center fielder even if you don't get a hit the rest of the year."

Before he got the chance to truly show the world, much less the Giants, the full scope of his talent on the field, Uncle Sam called the rookie into World War II.

The club felt the pinch in his absence, falling into a distant second place after holding a 2 ½ game lead on first. The following season, they lost 84 games and dove into fifth place.

Coaches and loyal fans pinned all their hopes for a return to glory on Mays military discharge, which came in the spring of 1954.

Chatter about Mays' return was so boisterous and rampant within the club at spring training in Arizona, that New York Herald Tribune sportswriter Roger Kahn was prompted to write the following sarcastic editorial. Incidentally, Kahn had never seen Mays play before the article ran February 29, 1954.

"Willie Mays is due to arrive in the Giant camp on Tuesday, not a day too soon. By Wednesday, half the Giant party will have left the desert sun, flown to Cooperstown, and started remodeling the Hall of Fame to include ten busts and five portraits of Willie.

"It's only human to wonder whether this is man or superman coming to join the Giants. In my case, the wonder takes the form of questions, and after I asked every authority around the swimming pool where I hang out, a good picture of Willie Mays emerged.

"Willie is ten-feet nine-inches tall. He can jump fifteen feet straight up. Nobody can hit a ball over his head.

"[His] arms extend roughly form 151st street to 159th [the location of the old Polo Grounds of Manhattan, where the Giants once played]. This gives him ample reach to cover right and left as well as center field.

"Willie can throw sidearm from the Polo Grounds to Pittsburgh.

"[His] speed is deceptive. The best evidence indicates he is a step faster than electricity.

"Willie does more for a team's morale than Marilyn Monroe, Zsa Zsa Gabor, and Rita Hayworth, plus cash ...

"That's about all there is to Mays, except that every authority added, "And if you think that's something, wait till you see him.""""

The very next day, for the first time, Kahn saw Willie Mays.

Only a few hours after climbing off a cross-country, over-night flight just days after his military discharge, Mays took to the field in a scrimmage game.

Pinch-hitting in the fifth, working on only a few hours sleep during the flight, he belted a 400-foot homerun. In the 7th, he caught a long fly ball to deep right-center field, then threw a spear to first-base to catch the returning runner on a double play. On the next pitch, Mays caught another shot to deep center, 50 feet straight back from where he stood, grabbing it over his shoulder.

Kahn was stunned, beginning his next article, "This is not going to be a plausible story, but then no one ever accused Willie Mays of being a plausible ballplayer."

The former Chattanooga semi-pro athlete seemed to hold the rest of his career to that standard. He amassed 3,283 hits, 6,066 total bases, and 660 homeruns in a career he ended in 1973 at age 42. He was the National League Rookie of the Year and was named the MVP twice, in 1954 and 1965. He won twelve Golden Glove awards, played in 24 All-Star games – a league record – and played in four World Series. He led the league in batting one season, in slugging five seasons, and in steals four seasons. Mays was the first player to top 300 homeruns and 300 steals in a career and he still holds the record for the most putouts by an outfielder – 7,095. Cooperstown welcomed the legend into their halls in 1979.

Of the boy who broke into the game at the base of Lookout Mountain, legendary ballplayer Ted Williams said, "They invented the All-Star game for Willie Mays."

While Mays spent the 1950s drawing crowds to ballparks across the majors, the Lookouts teetered between greatness and extinction as the glory of a league championship was curtailed by the passing of a legend and waning fans.

Chapter Fourteen

The Best of Times

Lookout, Don Grate crosses the plate
to a throng of happy teammates.

Minor League Baseball's first 'Golden Era' ended in 1949, after 464 teams across 59 leagues drew 42 million fans out to the old ballgame that season.

The advent of air conditioning and television seduced fans to the comforts of a cool living room and the flickering picture of their favorite ball team.

In his documentary, <u>Baseball</u>, Ken Burns noted, "Leagues were folding like afternoon newspapers, sometimes in mid-season and attendance was tumbling toward nine million per year."

Joe Engel was overheard saying even he believed the one-two punch of air conditioning and the television would be the end of Minor League Baseball. But he continued to prosper, bringing record-setting players like Don Grate and Ellis Clary to town, winning his third Association championship, and boasting about managers like Cal Ermer.

Named after the former president, Calvin Coolidge Ermer led the Lookouts from 1952 to 1957, setting the record for consecutive years managing the Chattanooga ball club.

Born in November 1923 in Baltimore, Maryland, he knew at a young age baseball would be his calling. In 1942, at age 19, he started playing minor league ball for the Washington Senators farm system in Burlington, North Carolina.

After three years serving as a Marine in World War II, he returned to the states and to baseball, heading to Orlando, Florida and by mid-season in 1947, he managed the Charlotte, North Carolina club to a championship season.

He played a single game in 1947 for the Senators, stepping to the plate three times never to get a hit. He spent spring training with the major league team in 1948 before heading back to manage in the minors.

In 1950, he led Orlando to a pennant win, then repeated with the Charlotte club in 1951.

Coming off a two-pennant win streak, the 32-year-old Ermer came to Chattanooga to manage the Lookouts. He stayed in Chattanooga for six seasons, still the longest consecutive streak for one person to manage the Lookouts. In 1958, he left the club to manage Birmingham and would coach the Minnesota Twins for two seasons, leading the club to a second place finish in the American League in 1967.

"He was a good manager," said Roy Hawes, who played first base for the team in the 1950s. "He was strict, but he knew baseball. He was a good clubhouse manager and a good spokesman."

Ermer's dedication to the game and commitment to strict discipline was very evident in every game.

During one game, Ermer sent 21 separate batters to the plate against a pitcher notorious for being un-hittable.

"He told us that anyone who hit off the pitcher could hit again, but if we struck out we were out for the game," Hawes said. "Only one person got a foul tip."

Ermer coached the Southern Association All-Star team three times – 1953, 1955, and 1957.

Aside from his stern demeanor, Ermer was a great scout.

"He recognized talent; he brought in Bob Oldis to the club, who was one of the best catchers in the game," Hawes said.

Chattanooga didn't lack talent on the field in 1952. Major League veterans like Hawes and second baseman, Ellis Clary graced the infield. Outfielders, Don Grate and Ernie Oravetz swung mighty bats while Al Sima, Sonny Dixon, and Jim Pearce ruled the mound.

The club led the Association three times in 1952 – once on May 20th, then again on July 10th. When they grabbed the lead a third time on August 16th, they never let it go, defeating Little Rock to claim the Southern Association Championship in an 8-4 victory September 6th in front of 6,015 fans. By the third inning, the club held a 5-0 lead over the Arkansas team.

Undoubtedly, one of the most unlikely heroes of the 1952 team was Don Grate.

A native of Greenfield, Ohio, and alumnus of Ohio State University, the all-American basketball player, selected to play for the United States basketball team in the 1944 Olympics, spent 1945 pitching for the Philadelphia Phillies.

Hurling a 98-mile-per-hour fastball, he won seven of thirteen games and earned a 2.23 ERA for the Phillies farm team in Utica, New York.

By the end of the season, the pitcher threw a few games for the Phillies. The following season, he won 14 games for Utica before again heading to the majors. But his dream was dashed one day in Philadelphia after not properly warming up.

He threw a fiery sidearm and heard something pop.

Despite his best efforts, Grate couldn't overcome his sore arm. He pitched for several teams, all the while watching his strike out total taper. Clubs used the former big leaguer only in relief spots or as a pinch-hitter, certain his days on the field were done.

In 1951, Grate landed in Chattanooga, sitting on the bench waiting for someone to get injured or called up so he could fill the space on the field – if only for just a few games.

He got his chance.

A Lookouts outfielder left a game injured and Grate took his place both on the field and in the batting order.

"Then I got lucky," Grate told a reporter from "The Sporting News" in 1952. "The first two times up I hit in the hole and legged them out for inside-the-park home runs, and they never took me out of the outfield."

While playing Nashville during the 1952 pennant drive, Grate showed Ermer and Engel what his arm could still do, throwing a peg to home plate from centerfield in the fog to save a tied game.

Though he'd returned to the starting lineup, Grate still hadn't found his calling – his trademark.

During a game at New Orleans in 1952, the Lookouts were invited to participate in a pre-game attendance booster full of games and contests intended to attract a crowd.

Ermer told Grate to enter the long-distance ball throwing contest, but Grate said no. Ermer persisted and Grate caved in.

"Bob Oldis"
Oldis' middle and ring finger were fused together and locked straight but, "he could still fire a ball down to second base," according to former teammate Roy Hawes.

"I threw from centerfield in the old Pelican ballpark and the darn ball went over the press box," he said. "They couldn't measure it."

Never one to miss the opportunity to explore a new promotion, Engel offered Grate $200 if he could break the existing world record for the longest ball ever thrown by a professional ballplayer.

On the last day of the season, September 7th, after the Lookouts claimed the Association title, Grate took on the 426-foot, 9 ½-inch record set in 1910.

He threw twelve balls from centerfield toward home plate, the best landing at 434 feet, 1 inch: a new world record.

At the end of the 1953 season, before a doubleheader with Little Rock, Grate tried again. After five throws, he set a new record of 443 feet, 3 ½ inches.

As his fame grew, Ermer took Grate and the Lookouts to play exhibition games and made him throw for the fans. On one trip, Grate's legendary arm was the only difference between freedom and jail.

Ermer took the club to play a game at the federal prison in Atlanta, but the prison authorities kept the Lookouts from leaving until Grate could throw a ball from the playing field high enough up the prison wall to break a window.

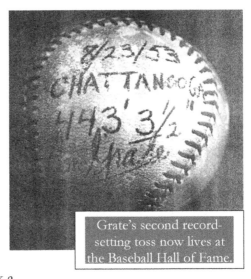

Grate's second record-setting toss now lives at the Baseball Hall of Fame.

"So I threw one," he said, "and it hit one of the dividing bars that separate the window panes. The guard said, 'You're going

118

to have to throw another one.' I threw that one on top of the prison and the let us all go home."

After leaving the Lookouts, Grate hurled yet another record long ball while playing for Minneapolis: 445 feet, which landed inside a fan's golf bag. His record was broken at the end

of the next season, when Canadian ,Glen Garbous threw a ball 445 feet, 10 inches.

In 1957, Grate said goodbye to baseball, certain Minneapolis' parent team – the New York Giants – likely wouldn't call him to the pros as long as former Chattanooga Choo Choo, Willie Mays was in their outfield.

Back in Chattanooga in 1952, aside from strong players, Engel assembled a crack staff to support his players to a championship.

Ruby Williams, the concessions manager at Engel Stadium, also fashioned sweat suits for the players to use during spring training in Winter Garden, Florida.

"She sewed rubber bands into the wrists and ankles of the suits," Hawes said. "You'd pull those rubber bands open and water would literally pour out your sleeves."

The team trainer, Davis "Sandy" Sandlin, started with the team in the 1930s, training the ballplayers. In the off-season, he worked as the trainer for the University of Chattanooga Moccasins football team.

"BellSouth Park should have been named Sandlin Stadium," Hawes said. "He devoted so many years to the team and to the Moccasins. Even after I quit playing, I'd still go back to him when I had a backache or something and he always treated me."

Sandlin's wife, Eleanor, was Engel's secretary from 1931 through 1965. She handled public relations for the club, tax reports, payroll, tickets and ticket sellers, bills, scrapbooks, sales options, contracts, suspensions and releases, just to name a few. Many said Eleanor was the woman who put Joe Engel's words into action.

In the early 1950s, Engel brought Paul Herman to the stadium to play the organ during the games, making Engel Stadium one of the first minor league parks in the country to feature an organist. Herman would go on to have an apprentice – Charlie Timmons – who continued playing the organ at Lookouts games until 1997.

Despite dwindling national interest in Minor League Baseball, Ermer and Engel kept the Lookouts on the front page in Chattanooga through the early 1950s.

In large part, the men owe a lot to one Shiloh, Illinois boy who invested his career in the Lookouts and his heart in Chattanooga.

Chapter Fifteen

The Love of the Game

Roy Hawes kisses his bride during a double-header on their honeymoon night.

When the 1952 Chattanooga Lookouts dominated the Southern Association, a humble Mid-Western boy with major league dreams was playing first base.

Roy Hawes won't tell you just how important he was to the team's success but his statistics will. The left-handed batter swatted .276 that season through 153 games and led the league in RBIs, piling up 93. During the championship game against Little Rock, he hit an impressive triple against the right field wall driving in a run and increasing the Lookouts' lead to 5-0. On the field, he helped turn two double plays leading to the club's victory.

By the time he came to Chattanooga, Hawes was no slouch.

When he returned from his two-year tour of duty with the United States Navy in 1946, the boy from Illinois turned his attention to playing Major League Baseball.

The spring of 1947 found Hawes playing Class D baseball in Texas. He spent the next five seasons playing Bush League ball in Texas, Indiana, and Oklahoma, where players played for little more than the chance to swing a bat for one more day.

"One time we took a collection on the team bus to get something to eat. Between all of us, we had 19 cents. So we stopped the bus by an apple orchard and hopped the fence, filling our pockets full of apples so we'd have something to eat," Hawes recalled.

Getting back on the bus was rarely a dream come true for the group of aspiring major leaguers. The team manager drove and, according to Hawes, "our bus was so old, I think they used it to take the first miners to the gold rush in California."

The bus was so weak, the players had to get out and walk beside it when going up hills, but the meager pay and raggedy travel conditions didn't deter Hawes.

He was determined to play until he couldn't play anymore.

That day almost came in 1950.

While batting for the Vincennes Velvets at a game in Mattoon, Illinois, Hawes was hit in the head with a pitch and knocked unconscious.

"We didn't wear helmets in those days and during the ambulance ride to the hospital, I kept going in and out of consciousness. When the ambulance turned left, I woke up. When it turned right, I'd pass out."

After a few days in the hospital, Hawes was released and he hitchhiked to the next town to catch up with his teammates, who'd gone on to play their next game.

He was admittedly gun-shy at his next trip to the plate, despite a teammate fashioning a crude helmet by putting cardboard in his ball cap.

"I think it made me a better ballplayer," Hawes laughed. "I learned to watch the ball better, I'll tell you that."

Years later, Hawes spoke with the catcher of that fateful game, who told Hawes he never meant for the pitcher to hit him.

"He said, 'I just meant for him to dust you off the plate a little. The pitch just got away from him'."

"Run for Run"

Of all the homeruns Roy Hawes hit during his 14-year career, he was robbed of one and gifted another.

During a Class D ballgame in Oklahoma, Hawes team was forced to play an away game in a "substitute ballpark" because the hosting team's park was under renovations.

"The park was in horrible shape," he said. "The grass was tall and the pitcher's mound was short. The pitcher kept throwing the ball too high to compensate for how low it was.

"When I hit a 145-foot shot down the third base line, it got lost in the tall weeds. While the other team was looking for the ball, I scored an inside-the-park, 145-foot homerun."

The baseball fates stepped in a few years later to even the score, during a game at Memphis while Hawes played for Chattanooga.

Memphis played on a football field, with home plate backed into a corner end zone. The right field wall stretched only the width of the football field – a few hundred feet – while the left field wall stretched the entire length of the football field – 100 yards.

In a game played the night before the Lookouts arrived to play, umpires ruled all balls hit over the right field wall would be ruled as a ground-rule double, regardless of the distance.

"They'd decided it was just too easy to hit a homerun," Hawes said. "The night before, everyone hit one."

But when Hawes smacked the ball so far over the right field wall it left the park, the umpires ruled the hit a ground-rule double, despite the distance.

"Since I hit the ball out of the park, I argued the call but they didn't give it to me," he said. "I guess that makes up for the one I hit into the weeds."

Losing consciousness didn't cause Hawes to lose his ambition and, by the end of the following season, his dedication paid off.

For four or five weeks during the 1951 season, the young ballplayer noticed a Cuban scout following the team from town to town, keeping his eye on Hawes during every game. By the end of the fifth week, the scout – representing the Washington Senators – bought Hawes' contract in exchange for four players and some cash.

"I didn't walk to the majors, I floated," Hawes said. "I was living every man's dream."

Hawes' time donning the Senators uniform lasted only a few months.

He played just three games, seeing six at bats and getting one hit, posting a major league career average of .167.

By the spring of 1952, Hawes was one of five first basemen trying out for the Double A Chattanooga Lookouts at spring training in Winter Garden, Florida.

Joe Engel saw that Hawes had natural talent and he became the obvious choice for first base.

In his first year with the Lookouts, Ermer led the club to win the Southern Association pennant. Hawes led the league in RBIs and, the following season, tied the record for most triples hit in a single game – three. Del Friar set the record in 1947, which has since been matched by Ivan Calderon in 1983 and Paul Hollins in 1986.

Hawes stayed with the Lookouts until 1956, leading the league in RBIs a second time in 1954.

But it wasn't always business on the field. There was plenty of time left for horseplay.

As the team gathered for pictures on the field one day, a feisty Hawes decided to play keep away with major league veteran Ellis Clary's ball cap.

"Clary was sensitive about his bald head and I don't know why I did it, but I did," Hawes said. "He took a powerful swing at me and I ducked. He said I was lucky I ducked and I said I was lucky he didn't hit me."

During one season, Hawes dodged a mighty swing from the right hand of justice due to some unpaid parking tickets.

Each day at baseball practice, Hawes parked his car wherever he pleased outside Engel Stadium. After practices, he'd toss aside any parking tickets left on his windshield.

Fans often packed the wooden bleachers along the outfield wall at Engel Stadium.

"I couldn't tell you why I did it now," he said. "We were ballplayers and we thought we were invincible."

A summons to appear in court because of his unpaid parking tickets brought Hawes back to the ground. In a matter of days, Roy found himself standing in front of the judge – Wilkes T. Thrasher – guilty as charged.

"[Thrasher] sat with Engel at all the games and he asked me, 'You haven't been doing too well recently, have you?' He was right," Hawes laughed. "I'd gone about zero for twenty and anything I did hit seemed to go right into somebody's glove."

The judge told Hawes he'd make the ballplayer a deal.

If the first baseman got two base hits in the game that night, he would forgive the parking tickets. But if he didn't, Hawes faced jail time for his offenses.

When he got to the field that night, Hawes was swinging for his freedom and Thrasher, like an angel of justice, sat high above the field behind home plate with Joe Engel at his side and watched.

At his first trip to the plate, Hawes singled, relieving some of his tension now knowing he only needed one more hit before he was home free.

But when his second and third trips to the plate ended in quick outs and a long walk back to the bench, he started to sweat.

Late in the game, after the Lookouts cycled through the batting order, Hawes took his fourth trip to the plate – his final for the night. He was all too aware this hit had to count or he'd spend the night in the county jail.

His hopeful swing connected bat with ball and the young ballplayer's heart leapt as the outfielder uselessly chased the ball until it sailed over the wall for a homerun.

"I remember hitting home plate, then looking up at Engel's box," Hawes told me. "I looked at that judge, pointed at him and said, 'You …' Then I pointed ant myself and said, '… and Me. We're even.' He just leaned forward and tipped his hat.

"I felt so relieved because, before that, I really thought I was going to jail."

Not every day at Engel Stadium featured Hawes with his back against the wall. He paired up with fellow player, Frank Sacka, who proved to be a good friend and just the kind of guy you'd want by your side when jumping into a fray of men scrapping for money.

One of Engel's zany promotions was Money Mondays.

At select Monday games, Engel put a wheelbarrow by the pitcher's mound and each fan would put a little pocket change inside. Then, before the game started, one lucky fan would win the wheelbarrow and all the treasure.

126

But there was a catch.

The winner had a set amount of time to get the wheelbarrow – now overflowing with change – off the field before a bell rang and the players cleared the benches, allowed to keep whatever they could grab.

For obvious reasons, the winner shuffled off the field in a frantic but determined manner, sloshing coins from left to right, certain to get off the field and keep most of his spoils before the players ran onto the field. Most winners left behind a trial of glittering goodies for bright-eyed ballplayers.

"There were some quarters and silver dollars in the tub but you can bet most of those coins were nickels," Engel said.

> "Fourth Time's a Charm"
> During one particular series, Felipe Montemayor – a Cuban player who spoke little English – hit a homerun to win the game. The next night, the opposing pitcher thanked Montemayor by hitting him with pitches each of his three trips to the plate - once in the arm, the next in the ribs, and a third time in the leg.
> When Montemayor's fourth trip to the plate came round, he stayed on the bench.
> The coach called Montemayor to head to the plate, but Montemayor said, "No."
> When the coach asked why, the player simply said, "Me sick."
> "He'd decided he didn't want to get hit anymore that night," said Hawes.

On other days, Engel scattered cash around the mound – singles, fives, tens, and twenties – and gave one lucky fan a time limit to grab as many as he could before clearing the benches.

It was during one of these dollar days that Hawes and Sacka made a pact on the bench. The pair of players would join forces – Sacka blocking while Hawes grabbed money with a fevered passion.

"We left the field with thirty dollars a piece that day, which was a lot of money because we only made $500 per month," Hawes said.

More than money, RBI records, and pennant wins, Hawes found his most prized moment through the game of baseball.

After being introduced through a mutual friend, Don Grate, Roy Hawes married Jeanie Baxter, a Ringgold, Georgia girl who worked at the DuPont textile factory.

The couple wed on August 9th, 1952 and, that night, Hawes joined the Lookouts in a doubleheader against the New Orleans Pelicans at Engel Stadium.

In the bottom of the ninth of the first game, with his bride dressed in her Sunday best, Hawes hit the game-winning homerun.

"I had some divine help on that one," he said.

After rounding the bases and tagging home, he headed straight for the stands where he kissed his bride.

"Someone took a picture of that and we had it enlarged," Hawes said. "It's hanging in my den with my jersey and the baseball bat."

Hawes first date with his future bride landed him in the hot seat with Engel.

"I came home thirty minutes late for curfew after that date and, the next day, Engel called me in to his office," Hawes said. "He said he had to tell the newspapers that I was late and that he'd have to fine me $100."

Facing a twenty-percent dock in his monthly salary, Hawes pleaded his case.

"I told him that was a lot of money and I couldn't afford that."

Apparently, Engel had a soft spot for lovebirds because he granted Hawes a pardon.

"He told the paper that I was fined, and the paper said I'd been fined, but he never fined me."

After that, Hawes was never late.

The remainder of Hawes' baseball career was littered with close calls and tough breaks. In 1956, he left Chattanooga for the recently acquired Triple A Senators club in Louisville, Kentucky. After a good year, the Philadelphia Phillies bought his contract and called him back to the majors. However, in an overnight trade, they acquired another first baseman from another major league team and decided they wouldn't need Hawes after all. The next morning, he caught a train to Triple A Miami.

In Miami, he met up with the legendary Satchel Paige who was eagerly awaiting his trip to the major leagues. Hawes had barnstormed with Paige for one week in the late 1940s, and the reunion was a welcome one.

"Paige would come into play about the 8th inning to finish the game after he'd been out fishing all day or something like that," he remembered. "He never had to warm up. His arm was ready to go at all times."

"He could throw a ball and knock over this glass," Hawes said, motioning to a glass of water during his breakfast at a local restaurant. "That's how amazing his accuracy was."

In 1958, Hawes saw his last close call with the majors when the Detroit Tigers brought his contract and moved him to Triple A Charleston, West Virginia. He stayed for a season, waiting for the majors to call but relying on some of the greatest players in the game to step aside and give him a chance.

The day never came.

In 1959, the Chattanooga Lookouts brought his contract back and the following season – when the Senators pulled their affiliation from the Lookouts and Joe Engel helped the city run the ball club – Hawes called it quits.

"I wanted to spend some time with children and my wife," he said.

For the next 50 years, Hawes immersed himself in his family and a sales career in the chemical industry. Today, he owns Dixie Trophy with his son, Greg, who played a season of Minor League Baseball with the Pittsburgh Pirates organization as a catcher.

His daughter, Lynn, pursued a career in softball through college but his granddaughter, Christi, has her hopes set on a different sport.

"She's a junior in high school and she plays golf," Hawes beamed. "She's already being looked at by colleges for scholarships. The other day, she shot a 72. I can't shoot a 72 without cheating."

> ### "You're Outta Here!"
> During a game, umpire Deacon Delmer called Danny Murtaugh out at first base.
> "Most of the time, players are dramatic when they're called out anyway but Murtaugh went over the top," said fellow Lookout, Roy Hawes.
> Murtaugh began shouting, "Out? Out?!", then grabbed his chest and fell to the ground.
> The umps response?
> or alive, Murtaugh, you're still outta here!"

Though he's been out of the game for nearly half a century, he has no regrets.

"In 1960, the Los Angeles Dodgers offered me a job managing one of their Class D clubs but I turned it down," he said. "I'd spent all the time I wanted in D ball. I didn't want to go back."

Though he can never go back, the Lookouts will be forever grateful Roy Hawes came to play.

Chapter Sixteen

Dark Clouds with Silver Linings

During spring training of 1954, Chattanooga was thrust into the middle of the national racial integration debate.

General Manager Zinn Beck took the Lookouts to Winter Garden, Florida for spring training, toting seven black Cuban players that signed with the team. The police chief told Beck, "We don't allow our Negro boys to play out there." Concerned for their safety, Beck sent those seven players to Orlando to train with the Washington Senators but word shot to the nation's capital like heat lightning.

Attorney General Herbert Brownell, Jr., cited the incident as a stark example of the nation's race problems. Clarence Mitchell, the director of the National Association for the Advancement of Colored People, accused the law enforcement in Winter Garden of giving "some free service to the Communist propaganda mill." Even President Dwight D. Eisenhower weighed in on the matter, tying the Winter Garden events in with Cold War tensions when he said, "We must constantly remember that the struggle against foreign tyranny can scarcely be won by an people who lightly regard their own people."

Following FBI attention to the matter, the Winter Garden city council issued a formal apology to the Lookouts, guaranteeing no harm would ever fall on any of the team members.

The incident marked the only time the federal government turned its attention to race relations in organized baseball in the South.

Despite being in the forefront of the progressive racial argument, the Lookouts' short-lived prominence in the national political arena did little to save the club or its parent affiliate – the Washington Senators – through the next decade.

At the end of the 1955 season, Clark Griffith died.

The Washington Senators organization landed in the hands of Griffith's adopted son, Calvin, who insured the slow death of the Chattanooga Lookouts.

From 1955 to 1960, the Senators finished last four times and the crowds were sparse. Calvin blamed low attendance on D.C.'s predominately African-American population, which seemed to ignore Senators games despite packing Griffith Stadium for Negro League games.

Calvin started shopping a new idea among the team's other owners, trying to drum up support for a move to Minneapolis, Minnesota – a city he deemed to be a better baseball town.

His initial suggestion was met with vehement opposition. The other owners refused to talk about it and many national politicians threatened to ignore legislation to help baseball, like the anti-trust exemption, if the Senators left Washington.

Still mourning the loss of his good friend, Engel was also adamant against Calvin's suggestion to move the club. After all, Engel spent his youth as a batboy and mascot for the club, then as a player, and a scout for another 15 years. He had never known a time without the Washington Senators by his side.

In August 1957, in an effort to try to liquidate the organization's assets and raise money for a potential move to Minnesota, Calvin put Engel Stadium up for sale with a half million dollar price tag.

However, Calvin masked his intentions when speaking to the media.

"Insurance and taxes are killing us," he told local reporters. "If we could sell [the park] to the city, as many owners are doing throughout the country, we could be spared the taxes."

Though Calvin was lobbying to move the organization from Washington, local interest in the Lookouts couldn't have been higher.

At the start of the 1957 season, Mayor P.R. Olgiati and Hamilton County Judge Wilkes T. Thrasher signed a proclamation declaring Opening Day at Engel Stadium a city holiday, requiring all workers receive a half-day off work to attend the game.

That season, one player would not disappoint.

The year before he died, Clark Griffith sent scout Ossie Bluege to Payette, Idaho, to report back on a teenage slugger named Harmon Killebrew.

On a spring day, Bluege watched a semi-pro game between two Idaho-Oregon Border League teams. When Killebrew stepped to the plate, he brought with him an .847 batting average and twelve consecutive hits – four homeruns, three triples, and five trips down the first base line.

> "Down the Third Base Line"
> Chattanooga 9-1-1 Dispatcher Al Graham recalled going to the ballpark in the late 1950s with his grandfather, who owned season tickets. "We'd always sit down the third base line, right behind the visiting team's dugout, so we could heckle the players and the umpire. I was only five or six at the time, but I'll never forget going to those games."

Intrigued, Bluege likely leaned forward as the pitcher rifled the ball toward the plate. Killebrew's swing carried the pitch 435 feet for yet another homerun!

The scout's wire to Griffith said of Killebrew, "The sky's the limit" and Griffith agreed, offering the 17-year-old powerhouse $30,000 for three years of play. When a scout for the Boston Red Sox refused to best the offer, Killebrew was D.C. bound.

Looking at Killebrew, there was no question about how he could swat a ball out of the park. The all-state high school quarterback came from a long line of strong men. His father was a fullback for his college football team and some said his grandfather – a Civil War soldier – was the strongest man in the Union army.

Despite his muscular physique, Killebrew struggled when he reached the majors. In his first few years in the big leagues, he couldn't establish a rhythm with the pitchers and his powerful bat was rendered useless.

In 1954, his first year as a Senator, Killebrew went from an .847 average to .308, hitting only four of thirteen times in nine games. Likely crediting Killebrew's slump to his first taste of the majors, Griffith brought Killebrew back the next season.

However, 1955 was the first season of Killebrew's four-season slump.

Killebrew

That year, his batting average slipped to .200, as he hit for only 16 of 80 trips to the plate in 38 games, amassing four homers, seven RBIs, and a double.

No longer impressed with their purchase, the Senators sent Killebrew to Single A Charlotte, North Carolina. Back in the minors, Killebrew relaxed and found his bat once again. Through 70 games he hit 81 times of 249 trips to the plate – swatting 16 doubles, seven triples, 15 homeruns, and 63 RBIs, to boast a .325 batting average.

Relieved their young slugger was clearly on the rebound, Washington called him back up only to be disappointed. Back in front of big league pitching, Killebrew faltered, hitting 22 of 99 trips to the plate and watching his average slide to .222.

Determined to give the muscle-bound third baseman some time to grow, the Senators sent Killebrew to Double A Chattanooga in 1957.

"I ran into Harmon on his way back down from the majors the first time," recalled former Lookout first baseman Roy Hawes. "He told me, 'I won't be here long. I've only hit six homeruns in six weeks and two RBIs. They won't keep me hitting like that. I just can't hit the pitching up here.'"

Killebrew's second trip to the minors proved as fruitful as the first as he quickly became one of the all-time greatest Lookouts players. Through 142 games, he hit 145 times off 519 at-bats. He scored 90 times, hit 30 doubles, seven triples, 101 RBIs, and 29 homeruns.

One homerun set a record that was never broken at Engel Stadium. Killebrew hit a ball 471 feet, straight over the centerfield wall – the only ball to clear the deepest centerfield in the history of the game.

Without hesitation, the Senators gave Killebrew his second chance at the majors, hoping he would bring his impressive display as a Lookout to the nation's capital.

It wasn't to be.

When Harmon returned to the majors, he struggled to continue his performance. In nine games, he hit for only nine of 31 trips to the plate, claiming two doubles, a pair of homeruns, and five RBIs, posting a .290 batting average.

The Senators saw he still didn't have enough power to compete at the major league level but refused to throw in the towel just yet. The next season, to the Lookouts' delight, Killebrew returned to the Scenic City donning Chattanooga's uniform.

The 1958 season was his most impressive since Charlotte in 1956. Killebrew hit 92 of 299 trips to the plate through 86 games.

He scored 58 times, hit 17 doubles, one triple, seven homeruns, and 54 RBIs, boosting his average to .308.

While the slugger had a monster year in the Scenic City, the Senators were fearful of being spurned by Killebrew a third time, so they sent him to Triple A Indianapolis.

Though his batting average dipped to .215 through 38 games, he remained fairly consistent, slapping five doubles, one triple, two homeruns, and ten RBIs.

By the end of the 1958 season, Washington called him back from the minors for the third, and possibly final, time.

Through thirteen games, he hit just six of 31 trips to the plate and his average dipped again to a dismal .194.

But Calvin Griffith must have seen a change in the Idaho native's attitude – something in his eyes or his demeanor or in the way he approached the plate or talked in the clubhouse – because he kept Killebrew for one more season.

And in 1959, the Senators investment paid off.

Through 153 games he hit 132 of 546 trips to the plate, swatting 20 doubles, two triples, 42 homeruns, and 105 RBIs!

His first homerun came in the season opener and during the season, he had five two-homer games. Forty two homeruns was enough that season to tie Rocky Colavito of Cleveland for the American League homerun title.

While some may have expected the season to be no more than a fluke, it definitely was not. For the next 14 seasons, Killebrew's season homerun total dipped below 25 only once, and he hit 49 total homeruns in 1964 and 1969. Killebrew played in the

All-Star game in 1959 and 1961 – then every season from 1963 to 1971. In 1969, he was voted the American League's Most Valuable Player and won the Lou Gehrig Award in 1971.

During his career he shared two American League homerun crowns and claimed four outright.

Killebrew's homeruns weren't of the spearing line-drive variety, rather "high, majestic pokes that invited measurement by public relations people," according to the National Baseball Hall of Fame.

Roy Hawes remembered the stark contrast between the struggling minor leaguer he'd talked to in 1957 and the record-setting slugger the nation watched through the 1960s.

"I wish I couldn't hit big league pitchers like he said he couldn't," Hawes recalled.

In 1975, the Minnesota Twins retired Killebrew's playing jersey – the same year he retired after a single season with the Kansas City Royals.

"The artificial turf took it out of my legs and I wanted no more of it," Killebrew said.

After his retirement, the former Lookout returned to the West, dabbling in cattle ranching, founding an insurance-securities business, and getting into sports broadcasting. In 1984, the Baseball Writer's Association of America voted Killebrew into the National Baseball Hall of Fame.

Without a doubt, Killebrew was the last good thing to come to Chattanooga because of the Washington Senators. When the Lookouts moved to BellSouth Park in 2000, leaving Engel Stadium to stand vacant, no one had bested Killebrew's homerun shot over the centerfield wall.

Likely, no one ever will.

Chapter Seventeen

1959: Cheaters, Pink Slips, and Passion

Without question, the single most definitive season in Lookouts baseball came in 1959.

As Chattanoogans rose to celebrate Independence Day, they were shocked by the lead story in Chattanooga newspapers. Two Lookouts players were suspended for failing to report a bribe by a gambler earlier in the season.

Southern Association President Charles Hurth made the announcement, stating it would be awhile before all the facts of the case were made clear and a decision would be reached.

While the suspension of Waldo Gonzalez had a minor impact on the team, fans were shocked by the suspension of the Lookouts' all-time homerun leader, Jess Levan – Harmon Killebrew's former roommate.

Levan had seen three trips to the majors so far, once with the Phillies in 1947 for two games and twice more with the Senators in 1954 and 1955 for 23 games. At his last trip to Washington, he'd hit three of his 16 trips to the plate, one of which was a homerun. There was no doubt this budding minor leaguer showed potential, carrying a major league career batting average of .286.

Engel graciously complied with the investigation, as did manager John "Red" Marion. Lookouts fans patiently waited for the outcome of the investigation while the media debated the issue on editorial pages every day for a month. No one was prepared for the judge's verdict when announced on July 31st.

Gonzalez, found guilty of no initial wrongdoing, was suspended for a year after being charged with efforts to obstruct the League's investigation into the matter.

Levan didn't fair so well.

During the trial, Lookouts pitcher James Heise testified against Levan, stating he had asked Heise whether he wanted to "make a little money" by throwing soft pitches to opposing batters. Heise declined the offer twice and other players stepped forward making similar claims against Levan.

The judge charged Levan with acting as a liaison agent for betting interests and offering fellow club members money to throw games. For his crimes, he was banned from the game of baseball for life.

"I'm quite sure I would have made a career in baseball," he told a Chattanooga reporter in 1989. "I was well-thought of in Washington, and after all that I had the prospects of going into coaching. I was bitter for a long time, no question. It ruined my life."

Chattanoogans debated the trial for a month, some finding the decision fair and others claiming the penalty was too severe. Still others hailed the quiet cooperation of Engel and the rest of the club's management, all of whom chose to not speak publicly of the accusations until after the decision was announced. At that time, Engel said that he thought it was the only answer the judge could come to if indeed the crimes had been committed. Marion echoed those sentiments.

The local press had little time to spend too much ink on the issue before yet another punch landed square on the jaw of Chattanooga baseball.

While attention was focused squarely on the trial of Levan and Gonzalez, Calvin continued to lobby for moving the Senators to Minnesota.

Joe Engel, coming off a semi-recent league championship and still boasting strong attendance numbers, misinterpreted his importance to the Senators organization. When the two strong-willed men collided, disaster was eminent.

Though no one can say for sure, the end of Engel's three-decade legacy as the eccentric owner of the Chattanooga Lookouts ended because the Senators left D.C.

When the American League opted to expand in 1960, Griffith agreed to expand with them, planning to move the Senators to Minnesota where they would be renamed the Twins – referencing the twin cities of St. Paul and Minneapolis.

"Go Joe" Engel was honored at two separate games late in his career.

In 1949, Southern League President Charley Hurth gave Engel the key to a new car full of gifts from the fans while a crowd of 4,683 looked on. At Engel's 25th anniversary as leader of the Lookouts at a game in 1953, in front of an audience of 9,000, Engel was honored again and he gave back – giving a portion of the day's ticket sales to the Alhambra Shrine to help crippled children.

This threat likely infuriated Engel. Engel threatened to step down as the owner of the Lookouts, taking all of his promotional expertise and ballpark success with him, if such a move was made and Griffith called his bluff.

Little more than a month after the players' scandal was resolved, Calvin dropped a bomb on Engel Stadium. On September 3rd, Engel was notified by telegram that the Senators were getting rid of the Lookouts effective September 15th.

Engel had twelve days to close up shop and report for duty, in Florida, as the head of the Washington Senators Baseball School in Winter Garden.

"Washington is no longer interested in continuing to run the club," Calvin told the Chattanooga Times. "We are selling but we would be interested in continuing to operate the club on a working agreement if someone else owned it."

The move was part of Calvin's effort to liquidate his assets – sell all the Senators farm clubs – in an attempt to come up with enough money to pay for the club's move.

The 60-year-old Engel immediately went to work trying to find a new affiliate for the club, as he had twenty two years before in 1937. However, this time his efforts were selfless. Engel's contract stood with the Washington Senators. Regardless of which club took over the Lookouts, Engel would have to leave town with the Senators in twelve days.

Potential buyers from the New York Yankees and the Chicago White Sox clubs came to Chattanooga, considering purchasing the team. But the impressive annual attendance of 252,703 set in 1952 had slumped to an uninspiring 55,989 by 1959. Neither club had a Double A Minor League affiliate but both passed on the opportunity to bring Chattanooga into their farm systems.

Distressed by the situation, an emotional Engel gave pink slips to all of the Lookouts' staff except Ruby Williams and Eleanor Sandlin.

"The tragedy is that unless someone takes the park for baseball, the stands will have to be torn down to make the almost 13 acres available for industry or something," Engel told Chattanooga Times reporter George Short. "That's what's awful. A lot of longtime employees of mine will be out of jobs."

Engel spent most of his last days at the stadium with his good friend, Bill "Rawmeat" Rodgers, who managed the club in Engel's first year in 1930.

Rodgers tried to keep Engel laughing, saying, "Well, Joe, I started off in this town with you and here I am with you at the end."

Engel replied, "Tell them I've gone, won't be back – that I've struck oil in Brazil." He continued, "If I don't joke some about this, I'll start crying."

One not surprised about the dismal end was Engel's wife, Hallie – whom he married in April 1934 – who told reporters, "I always told Joseph that baseball would have to leave him; he'd never leave it and that's what has happened."

In an article, George Short pondered a deeper question. Not just how to say goodbye to Engel, of whom Short said was "the perennial jokester, a man to whom every day is Christmas and every night New Year's Eve." Rather, how to say goodbye to Engel Stadium, which stood at the precipice of extreme change – leaving behind capacity crowds and facing desertion.

"How do you say goodbye to baseball in general?" he wrote. "To the fun of opening days when 28 out of 30 seasons the largest Southern Association crowd was right here? Maybe you don't. You just store these memories deeper and hope you're just saying 'so long,' not 'goodbye'."

Chattanooga got the chance to say goodbye at the Lookouts last game of the season – September 7th – five days before the Senators pulled the plug on the Lookouts lifeline.

When veteran first baseman Roy Hawes popped up a high fly ball at 9:02 p.m. against the Nashville Vols, the game was over. Paul Herman sat at the organ playing "Auld Lang Syne" – Engel's last eternal New Year's Eve.

No one seemed to notice or care that the Lookouts lost both games of the days' doubleheader. All eyes were on Joe Engel. The crowd presented him with a petition, passed through the stands that night, featuring several hundred signatures reading, "Dear Joe, If this is the last game here we want you to know we appreciate all you've done."

No one could have known, but they surely weren't surprised to discover, Engel was just getting started.

Soon after the end of the season, he organized a committee of local men, along with Mayor P.R. Olgiati and Hamilton County Judge Wilkes T. Thrasher, to save Lookouts baseball for the sake of the youth.

"When a boy gets through playing baseball all day, he's too tired to get into trouble," Engel said, in support of his long-running Knothole Gang.

The men continued to meet, drafting the formation of the Lookouts Youth Foundation; a non-profit group that would maintain the stadium for use by both the Lookouts and city recreational youth events.

Calvin Griffith agreed to lease the stadium to any group willing to pay one dollar per year in rent and assume full responsibility for the taxes and cost of maintaining the stadium on November 28th, just two days before the December 1st deadline set by the Southern Association for a club to state whether they would field a team for the following season.

Before the announcement, Engel raised enough money, with community support, to purchase the club for the Senators asking price of half a million dollars. However, a move to purchase the club was blocked by the courts in Washington, D.C., which froze all the Senators assets – including the potential sale of the Lookouts to interested investors.

Apparently, a die-hard fan and minority-stock holder in the Washington Senators was suing Calvin and the Senators for moving out of D.C. – a move increasingly unpopular among residents of the nation's capital.

Chattanooga was left holding a pot of money and good intentions until the legal system decided to act.

When Calvin's offer to lease the building for a dollar came through late Friday, November 28th, Engel fled to Nashville for a deadline extension from the Southern Association as to whether baseball would be played in Chattanooga in 1960.

Meanwhile, Little Rock, Arkansas investor Ray Winder watched the proceedings with fevered interest. Winder was eager to bring a Southern Association affiliate to Little Rock and saw a great opportunity when he heard the Lookouts were up for grabs.

On Sunday, November 30th, with Engel unable to reach any Southern Association official over the weekend, the Senators relinquished control of the club to the Association. The Lookouts immediately became eligible to become the property of the highest bidder.

Engel's longtime friendship with League president Charles Hurth served him well. Hurth kept all other bidders at bay until he could speak with Engel and grant him a deadline extension. Engel reclaimed possession of the Lookouts under the ownership of the newly chartered Lookouts Youth Foundation and, for the second time in history, the club was locally owned.

Calvin agreed to let Engel stay on at Chattanooga and continue receiving payment from the Senators for the remaining years of his contract, as long as the Lookouts maintained a working agreement with Washington with regards to purchasing players. If, at any time, the Lookouts found a new major league affiliate Engel would have to choose to keep his $25,000-per-year job with the Senators or leave the organization and sign a new contract with the new affiliate.

Early estimates prepared by the Lookouts Youth Foundation cited the group's annual budget requirements between $100,000 and $200,000. The group knew immediately they would need at least $50,000 to even start operating the club independently.

On December 22nd, Engel led the charge to raise the funds. In little more than three weeks, the goal was met. By the end of January, a second group was chartered – the Lookouts Booster Club – and charged with operating the day-to-day business of the baseball team. The Lookouts Youth Foundation busied itself filling the calendar around the baseball games, using the stadium for youth baseball games when the Lookouts weren't playing and high school football games in the fall for schools without fields, such as Notre Dame and Howard high schools.

Every day except those 70 Lookouts games and Sundays were filled.

Without a major league affiliate, the club had no baseball players coming up from the lower leagues. The Senators sent most of the Lookouts 1959 team to Charleston, West Virginia. So Engel leapt into action once again, heading to spring training camps in Winter Garden, Florida, to beg for players.

By February 18th, Engel arranged for six members of the Pittsburgh Pirates farm system and a manager – Forrest V. "Spark" Jacobs – to come to Chattanooga. Members of the Lookouts Booster Club eagerly worked to secure a deal to receive a few players from the Philadelphia Phillies. Only three former Lookouts returned for the 1960 season, one of which was Roy Hawes.

While the staff and committee members of the two new chartered organizations scrambled to put a season

"Here's Your Sign"
During one particular lapse in attendance, Joe Engel hung a sign above the main gate reading, "This park is not quarantined."

together, the media and devoted fans urged the community to get involved. Frequent television specials and newspaper editorials stressed in no uncertain terms the only way the Lookouts would stay in Chattanooga in 1961 would be through heavy fan involvement and support.

Through mid-February, fans pledged to purchase between 20,000 and 25,000 season tickets. By the time game day rolled around on April 17th, 1960, newspaper reports estimated 13,000 to turn up at the ballpark to cheer on the downtown team snatched from the clutches of a seemingly imminent doom during the winter months.

When just 6,001 actually came to the game, in which Atlanta defeated the Lookouts, the Lookouts Booster Club blamed last-minute Easter shopping and thin wallets due to the national deadline for filing taxes.

However, the disappointment in fan attendance of the season opener seemed to set the bar for the rest of the year. By the end of 1960, the club posted a 16-year attendance low and finished 26 1/2 games out of first.

It marked the final season of a relationship between the Lookouts and the Washington Senators.

In 1961, the Senators became the Minnesota Twins. Gil Hodges and Ted Williams tried to manage a second Washington franchise but after just ten seasons, winning no pennants and drawing less-than-impressive crowds, owner Rob Short moved the club to Texas and renamed them the Rangers. Baseball didn't return to D.C. until 2005, when the Montreal Expos became the Washington Nationals.

Dark clouds loomed over Engel Stadium – a house without a master, a team without a parent club, a ship without a captain – as the futile countdown of Joe Engel's reign as the King of Baseball in the Scenic City began.

Chapter Eighteen

Getting the Philly of Things

For the next four seasons, Chattanooga struggled with the rest of the league to attract a crowd. Televisions grew in popularity and affordability, drawing fans home to watch their favorite major league game on the TV screen.

However the Lookouts forged ahead, finding a new major league affiliate in the Philadelphia Phillies and bringing to town a new manager, Frank Lucchesi. Engel ended his contract with the Senators, a relationship he'd maintained for four decades, and became an employee of the Phillies organization.

By the time the season started on April 12th, 1961, only 4,327 people came out to the old ballgame – a far cry from the 26,000 crowd that graced the stands in 1936.

But the players didn't seem to notice.

They beat the club from Macon, Georgia 12-3 and set the tone for the rest of the season on the field. By the fall, the

The 1961 club claimed the last pennant before baseball left Chattanooga.

Lookouts dominated the Southern Association with an impressive tenth-inning win over the Shreveport Sports 8-4 to claim the club's fourth Southern Association pennant – their first in nine years.

The commanding title victory was bittersweet.

Only 233 fans sat in the 10,000-capacity stadium to witness the win. Accounts in the Chattanooga Times featured tight-shot photos of celebrating players in the locker rooms and quotes from excited staff and representatives of the Phillies organization.

One can imagine the writers had a hard time finding a fan to talk to.

In late December, the struggling Southern Association disbanded, leaving behind only the Texas and Mexican leagues at the Double-A level, nationwide.

The announcement came to Chattanooga too late for the Lookouts to join play as part of the Single A South Atlantic League – the same league they played in when first coming to the Scenic City in 1909.

Chattanooga was a team without a league and,

> "Preaching to the Choir"
> After Engel paid for a young black man to go to seminary school, the young man returned to the ballpark to preach against the evils of playing baseball on Sunday. Engel replied, "Sunday baseball was where I got the money to send him through school."

thus, missed their first season of play in more than 50 years.

Adding insult to injury, the Lookouts Youth Foundation already signed another annual commitment to pay the annual taxes in the stadium - $4,500 – plus do the scheduled maintenance for the season though they had no baseball team to help generate an income.

Finally, the Phillies also chose to pull their affiliation with the Lookouts, despite the club winning the Southern Association title the season before. Phillies executives cited they needed only one Class A ball club, and chose to keep their team in Williamsport, Virginia.

Typical of his dedication to the club, Engel worked diligently to orchestrate the return of baseball to Chattanooga in 1963. His efforts paid off and, the following season, Sally League president Sam Smith made the league a Double-A contender with Chattanooga in tow.

Engel also brought Philadelphia back as an affiliate, though the major league club now called themselves the Nationals. In a statement to the media, Engel said, "This is no bull, we're back in the baseball business."

Long term success still depended on fan attendance and the Lookouts were optimistic.

"If everybody who asked me this year about next year's baseball will come out to the park, we'll break all sorts of records," said David Eldridge, city councilman, grounds superintendent for the Lookouts Youth Foundation, and Engel's close friend.

In an effort to boost attendance, the Lookouts made a decision. For the first time in the team's history, the club scheduled a night game for opening day in an attempt to give the largest number of prospective fans the opportunity to come.

When the Lookouts took the field at 7:30 p.m., they did so in front of a crowd of 8,215.

The crowd was part of a Lookouts first.

Though Cuban players donned the Lookouts uniform since the mid-1950s, the 1963 season marked the first season African-American ballplayers took to the field at Engel Stadium.

Four ballplayers – outfielders, Charley Fields and Adolfo Phillips and infielders, Bob Sanders and Harold "Hank" Allen – broke Chattanooga's color line.

The fully integrated club beat the Knoxville Smokies 5-4 in ten innings in front of the largest crowd since 1956. The team fared worse than their title season in 1961, but nothing could defeat the optimism of the members of the two chartered non-profit groups running the clubs.

The Lookouts Youth Foundation, set up to use any profit from operating the stadium for the benefit of youth recreation, posted a profit for the first time since its inception in 1960. However, the profit was deceptive.

The Foundation each year paid the Lookouts Booster Club approximately $4,500 for taxes and maintenance of the building. Ticket sales guaranteed an equal amount, keeping both groups at an even wash and the youth of Chattanooga still waiting for the anticipated financial windfall promised in the winter of 1959.

Things took a turn for the better in the Southern League in 1964. Sam Smith blended his Sally League with a few discarded members of the old Southern Association and founded the new Southern League, which still operates today.

Chattanooga struggled both on and off the field recording 16 consecutive losses to the Asheville Tourists. Engel called the players the worst he ever fielded.

One such player was Grant "Buck" Johnson.

Like fine wine, former Lookout "Buck" Johnson got better with age. At the young age of 21, Johnson came to pitch at Chattanooga, losing all three games he started and only pitching in four games that season. As a member of the Philadelphia Phillies farm system, he surely wondered if he'd ever see the majors while boasting a 9.64 ERA and lingering in the shadows of a future hall-of-famer.

However, by the end of the decade his pitching improved and he played in the 1969 All-Star game. He joined the Baltimore Orioles in their playoff berths in 1971, 1973, and 1974 and again with the New York Yankees in 1976. But it was 15 years after Johnson left Engel Stadium before he gave his best performance. In 1979, he led the Pittsburgh Pirates to a World Series win, pitching an impressive 2.96 ERA through 72 games! Johnson makes a good case for the phrase, "Good things come to those who wait."

The next season, 1965, the team finished in dire straights, twenty games out of first place behind Columbus, Georgia.

Dubbed the "Laughing Lookouts," they set a league record by striking out to pitcher, Bob Lasko, 15 times. They went 22 innings without scoring a single run. Asheville defeated Chattanooga 13 consecutive times, including the Lookouts' final game of the season – a 16-4 home game loss in front of a laughable crowd of just 355 fans.

The game was deemed, "Save the Lookouts Night," as the team fell to Asheville 7-1.

Al Raffo, who played on the team, blamed himself.

"Yeah, I did a lot myself to kill baseball in Chattanooga," he said. "That team, or the quality of that team, kept the people from coming to the ballpark. I think people here must have a winner before they support a team. That was definitely not a winning club."

One reporter stated simply that the team finished so far down in the standings, manager Andy Seminick used a periscope most of the year to catch a glimpse of the front runners.

At the end of the season, Philadelphia pulled their affiliation with Chattanooga for a second time. The Chicago White Sox toyed with the idea of taking over Lookouts baseball for two years but ultimately decided to pass up the club.

Amidst the gloom of the end of Chattanooga baseball, the Scenic City saw a last, fleeting glimpse of a shooting star in the form of a lanky Canadian named Fergie.

Chapter Nineteen

The Game is Easy, Life is Hard

Some might say Ferguson Jenkins was the last good thing to happen to the Chattanooga Lookouts in the 1960s.

Ferguson Jenkins might say that the Chattanooga Lookouts are the best and worst thing to ever cross his path.

The Canadian-born pitcher was a natural athlete. During high school, he lettered five times as part of the track, basketball, and hockey teams. Jenkins quit playing hockey after receiving 14 stitches in his head from the game.

The boy's love of baseball developed from his father – Ferguson, Sr. – who played semi-pro baseball with a segregated all-black team called the Black Panthers. Since Jenkins was tall and thin, he was groomed to play first base but later found an interest in pitching while throwing rocks into passing train boxcars.

His skillful arm and spot-on accuracy was undeniable and soon noticed by Philadelphia Phillies scout, Gene Dziadura. Dziadura worked with the high school student, training his arm for pitching, and his mind for baseball.

When Jenkins graduated high school in 1962, he signed a contract with the Phillies organization and was bound for warmer weather.

The last time any of Jenkin's relatives saw life south of the Canadian border was a century earlier. His mother's great grandparents were smuggled from the Confederate South during the Civil War along the perilous path of the Underground Railroad.

Jenkins returned to the South to be revered and applauded.

Trading maple leaves for palm trees, Jenkins went to Single A Miami, winning seven of nine starts and appearing in 11 games posting an ERA of 0.97! Obviously impressed, the club sent Fergie to Triple A Buffalo, New York – an overwhelming jump for the rookie ballplayer. He won only one of two starts in three games while watching his ERA spike at 5.54.

The start of the 1963 season, his ace-pitching arm returned to Miami and he won twelve of 17 starts and boasted a respectable 3.41 ERA.

For a second time, the Phillies thought Fergie was too advanced for Single A ball. One scouting report said Jenkins was "a Canadian veterinarian who can hold the horses. Control is his best asset. He has a chance to go all the way." They sent Jenkins to play at Triple-A Arkansas where, again, he floundered. He lost his only start in four games and posted a 6.30 ERA.

By the start of the 1964 season, he headed back to Double-A baseball into the arms of a struggling ball club standing on its last leg, joining the Chattanooga Lookouts.

From the start of the season to the first part of August, a 20-year-old Jenkins was a standout player amidst a field of otherwise forgettable faces. He won ten of 16 starts, playing in 21 games and pushing his ERA to 3.11. It was the first time Fergie kept his ERA around 3.00 since leaving Single A ball.

Though Chattanooga struggled through the 1964 season, personally Jenkins soared. The lanky Canadian led the Southern

Association in strikeouts at 147 and was named to the Association All-Star team. Proving he believed in the importance of being a batting pitcher, Jenkins also claimed a two-run homer on July 17th.

"When you go up to the plate, you become a batter," Jenkins said in an interview after his year with the Lookouts. "If you just stand there, you're a weak sister. But if you swing the bat, you're a dangerous part of the lineup."

Through his career, he broke .250 only once, amassing 148 hits off 896 at-bats through 450 games. He hit 13 career homeruns and 85 RBIs, proving he was much more menacing on top of the mound than facing it.

Impressed by the 20-year-old arm and Jenkins' ability to maintain a respectable ERA away from Single A clubs, the Phillies called him back to Arkansas where he was ready to stay. He started in 10 of 11 games, winning half, and posting a 3.16 ERA. In 1965, still in Arkansas, he gripped Triple A baseball and never let go, winning eight of 14 starts, and playing 32 games. His ERA was a commanding 2.95 – the lowest it had been since his minor league debut in 1962.

In midseason, he was called to the major leagues and dominated, playing with Philadelphia for two seasons, the Chicago Cubs for 10, Texas for six, and Boston for two.

During his 19-year career in the majors, he pitched a lifetime ERA 3.34. He won 284 games and lost 226 tallying 3,192 strikeouts. In six consecutive seasons, Jenkins won 20 games each year. From 1965 to 1983, his ERA slipped above 4.00 only three times. During those 18 seasons, Jenkins' ERA stayed below 3.50 for 12.

Fans loved and respected him, validating his appearance in three All-Star games from 1967 to 1972. In 1971, he won the National League's Cy Young Award. In 1974, Jenkins was named the American League Sporting News Comeback Player of the Year. In 1987, he was voted into the Canadian Baseball Hall of Fame and, in 1991, received the same honor as he was voted into the National Baseball Hall of Fame in Cooperstown.

Most who saw him pitch would say he was both unusual and exceptional because of his pitching style. He was not afraid of throwing strikes and was deadly with his accuracy. Of all the pitchers ushered into the 3,000-strikeout club, Jenkins is the only one to have sacrificed less than 1,000 walks.

"I tell youngsters to make the batter do half the work," he said. "Throw strikes. If the batter takes them, he'll strike out. If you don't throw strikes and give up a walk, you get angry with yourself, your catcher is disappointed, your manager is mad, and the pitching coach is unhappy."

Possessing the bravado to throw strikes is not without risk. Sometimes, a batter finds the strike. Jenkins leads the Cubs' all-time list for most homeruns allowed by a pitcher – 271 through 2,673 and two-thirds innings.

Despite his many triumphs, Jenkins suffered great losses.

In 19 years, Jenkins never once saw the postseason since he was never part of a winning team.

Off the field, he saw much of the same.

After his first marriage ended in divorce, Jenkins' second wife died in a car accident.

What seemed to be a bright spot in his life came in the winter of 1992. The Chattanooga Lookouts desperately sought a new pitching coach and thought of Ferguson Jenkins.

On December 1st, the local newspaper reported the great news: Jenkins was Scenic City bound.

"I haven't signed [a contract] yet because I went hunting but I will sign it," Jenkins told reporters while hunting in Kittaning, Pennsylvania.

When Jenkins returned home and shared the news with his fiancé, she violently objected. Three weeks later, still resolute against a move to Chattanooga, she climbed into the couple's car in the garage with their 3-year-old daughter and started the car. In hours, both died tragically of carbon monoxide poisoning.

In February, Jenkins sent word to Chattanooga that he could no longer accept the position as pitching coach. Instead, he would stay home and care for his remaining children.

It's no surprise Jenkins titled his autobiography, "The Game is Easy, Life is Hard."

"In my life, I've been part of many funerals. At one point, I told a reporter I should be in a rubber room," he said. "There are two things in baseball. Either you win or you lose. Life is like that, too. How you get through it depends on how strong your faith is."

Today, Jenkins is married to his third wife and operates his own charity – the Ferguson Jenkins Foundation, supporting charities of all kinds, from cancer to blindness.

The former Lookout definitely has a plan to win not only in baseball, but also in life.

Chapter Twenty

The Longest Winter

For a decade, the occasional snow was the only visitor at Engel Stadium.

In 1966, the inevitable happened.

Not with a bang, but with a fizzle, baseball left Joe Engel. Failing to attract a crowd, the club was forced to fold.

It was a fact the King of Baseball refused to accept.

The Lookouts Booster Club continued to operate Engel Stadium, using the interest accruing from the initial $50,000 investment raised in 1960. Engel demanded the ballpark stay ready to host another team at a moment's notice.

After two years of intense negotiations with the Chicago White Sox, Engel, the city council, and county commissioners, the discussions proved futile.

In front of a March meeting of the Lookouts Booster Club in 1966, Engel – now 73 years old – continued preaching optimism.

"I'm sure a major league club will want to put a farm team in Chattanooga because of our fine park," he said.

No one did.

The Booster Club's numbers were a dismal disappointment, unable to attract local fans to even local events, such as high school and little league games. Only 27,707 tickets sold in 1965, the final year the Lookouts fielded a team. Ticket and concession sales generated $121,000 - $21,000 under the necessary $142,000 to cover operational expenses and past debts.

For three years Engel tried all in his power to get baseball back into Engel Stadium but he was an old man in fading health. He was unable to hop trains to Nashville to make deals with league presidents or take red-eye flights to spring training camps in Florida to rustle up affiliates or players.

Calvin Griffith, now the proud owner of the Minnesota Twins, took pity on Engel and gave him a job scouting minor league prospects for major league potential within the Twins' organization.

Engel still held his offices at the stadium where he daily reported for duty. Some days, he invited his friends through the years – reporters, officials, ballplayers, and managers – to sit on his roof and watch cars pass along East Third Street.

"See those cars?" he once asked. " I've counted about 50 now in 10 minutes. And at least three out of every five is pulling a boat headed for the lake. That is the funeral procession for baseball here – everywhere – in the minors. Too much free time, too many free attractions that are new and fresh. Baseball can't keep the pace; too costly."

Forecasting the future, Engel would point to the outfield and tell his friends, "When I die, I want to be buried beneath the LOOKOUTS sign in centerfield and I want the band to play, 'Please Don't Talk About Me When I'm Gone.'"

In July 1968, Vice Mayor A.L. Bender made a move to have Engel's office preserved just as it was, forever.

"My son was amazed," Bender said, of the moment his 11-year-old walked into Engel's office and saw trophies, letters, pictures, relics, and momentous spanning more than three decades of Chattanooga baseball.

Bender, right, wanted to preserve Engel's unique office, left.

Bender said flatly that losing Engel's memories "would be a shame."

In the end, not only did Chattanooga not solely lose his memories, but also the legend himself.

In 1969, still scouting for the Twins, Engel fell ill.

For two weeks, nurses and doctors at Campbell General Hospital tended to the ailing Engel. On June 12th, 1969, a national pastime lost its legend.

William Joseph Engel died at age 76.

The following day, the front page of both competing newspapers – The Chattanooga Free Press and The Chattanooga Times – printed lengthy tributes to the man who had come to be synonymous with baseball and entertainment in the Scenic City.

"He was a prince of a guy," said David Eldridge's widow, Mary. "They didn't make them any better than Joe Engel. What he did for this city – particularly the young people – nobody but Joe Engel could know."

A city mourned.

The flag posted in outfield at the stadium bearing his now legendary name flew at half-staff.

"Joe Engel was a man of many interests, ambitions, desires and benefactors," wrote columnist E.T. Bales. "Of these, one could write a book, but not with his blessings. He neither wanted nor expected thanks for the things which he did for his friends, or the unfortunate of his neighborhood or community."

Whether Engel wanted praise was not at issue upon his death – he received it in abundance. Through the next three days, eight articles were printed featuring quote after quote from those who were affected by his life and his death.

"This is a sad blow for me," said Atlanta Crackers General Manager Earl Mann. "We had so many, many great times together. We battled each other so hard but we really loved each other. I guess we'd rather beat each other as anybody else in the league."

A few days after his death, Engel was buried at the foot of Lookout Mountain, at Forest Hills Cemetery (today,

Engel is buried at the base of Lookout Mountain.

at 4016 Tennessee Avenue) surrounded by a throng of mourners.

Six men carried the casket, including Cal Ermer, sportswriters Wirt Gammon and Allen Morris, and broadcaster, Luther Masingill. Forty-six others were listed as honorary pallbearers, including former players Fred Graf and Hillis Layne.

Baseball bats and autographed balls mixed in with graveside flowers and somber mourners that summer day. As Engel was returned to the earth from which we all come, many said

Chattanooga baseball immediately changed in the eyes of the nation.

"I think it was best said by a veteran baseball man in the recent baseball draft," said Ermer, at the funeral. "Since Joe's been out of running the Lookouts, you never hear about Chattanooga. When he ran the team, there was always a dateline coming out of Chattanooga and going all over the country."

A simple headstone reading 'ENGEL' marks his grave, five miles from the ballpark to which he dedicated his life.

Fourteen miles away sat his wife, in the couple's horse farm on Julian Road, left with the responsibility of handling his affairs. She agreed to continue the pursuit to bring baseball back to Chattanooga.

However her pursuit was short-lived. Just eight months after Joe died, Hallie Engel passed away – on February 26, 1970.

Upon her death, Engel's sister coordinated the collection of all Engel's trophies, scrapbooks, and photographs still in his office at Engel Stadium. The entire collection was donated to the National Baseball Hall of Fame on March 17, 1970.

Chattanooga was left with nothing but memories of the good old days and a decaying ballpark at the end of O'Neal Street.

Four months after Engel's death, the Cleveland Indians came to town, interested in buying the stadium and bringing to town another minor league franchise. But the Lookouts Booster Club no longer operated the grounds, drowning in tax bills they couldn't pay and repairs they couldn't make. The city took on the stadium under the umbrella of the Public Works Department and the county helped defray some of the costs but both were eager to unload the responsibility on a new major league affiliate.

Representatives from the Indian's organization waited for the city and county to make an offer wherein they would retain financial responsibility of the park and grounds. City council members and county commissioners patiently waited to hear the

Indian's plan to shoulder the financial burden of an aging stadium just as the Senators did during the glory days of Scenic City baseball.

Neither budged.

Estimates to repair the stadium, which stood vacant for half a decade, neared $50,000. The issue, as far as the city was concerned, came down to attendance.

"I can't see spending that kind of money for one year and have one hundred people see baseball," Mayor A.L. "Chunk" Bender told a representative from the Indian's organization during a city council meeting.

Both parties balked until the Indians gave up, opting not to bring their Double-A club to Chattanooga.

Engel Stadium remained empty for six more years, letting time pick away at the stands and wear on the field.

In 1969, both governments combined to pay $9,322.59 to maintain the stadium.

Eager to come up with some way to offset more costs, the city leased the park to the University of Chattanooga for five years in 1970, giving the school the option to buy. Generating some revenue through ticket sales to cut some of the expenses to the local governments, which paid $3,011.49 to operate events at the stadium in 1970.

In 1971, costs dipped again to $1,976.51. The city and county paid $2,128.64 in 1972 and $2,420.01 in 1973 as the level of disrepair mounted.

News Free Press sports columnist Allen Morris wrote, in 1972, that the park was the "Ghost Town building" stating, "paint is peeling off the walls and seats, the floors are filthy, the roof is falling down, and it looks like a tornado hit the place."

At the end of the five-year lease, the University chose not to purchase the stadium and the park reverted back to the complete care, and expense, of the city and county.

Vacant through all other months but a few in the spring, the stadium slowly crumbled.

By 1975, a local businessman and his wife, Woodrow and Sarah Reid, and their son, Mark, united with optometrist, Jim Crittenden, to start talks with the Oakland Athletics about bringing baseball back to the Scenic City after a decade-long drought.

Following a few visits to Engel Stadium from Athletics owner, Charles Finley, the club decided they'd bring their Double-A club to Chattanooga if the stadium were restored to its original glory.

Knowing the city and county's stance on lending money to a local baseball franchise, Reid chose to finance the renovations of the stadium himself, taking a loan for $150,000 to do the job.

"I remember Joe Engel and all his colorful stunts in Chattanooga in the past," Finley told local reporters. "I think the city ought to be ripe for baseball's return."

December 10th, 1975 marked the formation of the Engel Stadium Corporation, a business entity made up of the Reid family, Crittenden, and local attorney, Arvin Reingold, who served as treasurer and legal advisor for the group.

Throughout the winter of 1975 and the spring of 1976, Reid organized citywide stadium clean up days, which he named "Sparkle Days." Every able-bodied Chattanoogan was invited to come to the park to replace broken windows, paint the stands, and repair various other odds and ends in need of attention at the ballpark.

"It was no easy feat to peel away over ten years of neglect at Engel Stadium," wrote Harmon Jolley, who told of his memories in an article for TheChattanoogan.com. "The venue was in such bad shape that an inspection by Oakland A's farm director Syd Thrift and Southern League President Billy Hitchcock required crawling in through a window."

The new owners and management of the club headed to the park to put a new face on an old building. The Moccasin baseball team lent a hand and people from off the street, eager to see Engel Stadium restored to the days of glory, picked up hammers and paint brushes.

In March 1976, the newest members of the Lookouts ball club attended spring training in Mesa, Arizona. In April, the players came to Engel Stadium as the newest members of the Western Division of the Southern League. Woody Reid invited the city to come out and watch the team practice, charging just one quarter per person.

After 11 seasons without the crack of a bat or the roar of a Double-A crowd, the Lookouts returned to Engel Stadium on April 20th to the delight of all.

Chapter Twenty One

Going for Broke

After personally financing the $125,000 renovation of Engel Stadium, and another $25,000 to buy miscellaneous odds and ends like equipment, Woody Reid was ready to bring the Lookouts back to the ballpark.

More than 4,000 days – 11 years and three months –passed in the Scenic City since the last time a Lookout swung a bat, chased a ball, or threw a double play.

When the team arrived into town from spring training in Mesa, Arizona, hundreds turned out to Lovell Field to welcome them.

On opening day, the stadium buzzed with activity and anticipation as 8,305 fans waited to see the return of baseball to Chattanooga. Ushers took their post in the stands wearing Oakland's green and gold, matching the new color scheme of the stadium. Hillis Layne made his way to the park to see the Lookouts play; no doubt a better memory than standing at Engel's grave seven year before.

At the top of the stands, near the press box, sat a new face. Charlie Timmons, the apprentice of former Lookouts' organist Paul Herman, came to the park as part of a package deal.

When Reid approached Hammond Organs, a local organ retailer in town, about the prospect of donating an organ for use at the park, the owners agreed on one condition. Timmons, their employee, would play it.

Reid agreed and Timmons began a relationship with the Lookouts lasting nearly two decades.

When the players took the field, most eyes were fixed on the club's top prospect, Bob Mullenhauer. At the end of the 1975 season, before heading to Chattanooga, Mullenhauer was swinging an impressive .423 batting average.

However, by the time the game got underway, three other players stole the show.

Facing the Charlotte Orioles, the Lookouts played a ferocious game energized by the enthusiasm of the crowd. Eager to please, these Lookouts played as they never had before to please one of the largest minor league crowds any of them had ever seen – or maybe ever would.

> **"Ease" His Pain**
> In the 1950s, Joe Engel gave season tickets to the family of young Charlie Timmons. You see, Engel needed to run electricity to his horse farm on Julian Road, but the only way he could do that was to receive an easement from the Timmons family who owned property between Engel and his source of electricity. So, in exchange for a 'right-of-way' through the Timmons' property, Engel traded tickets to the ol' ball game, thus starting the beginnings of a long relationship between Charlie and the Lookouts.

Mark Budaska had a huge night at the bat, smacking a 365-foot grand slam, which pulled the Lookouts into a 5-1 lead. Later, he smacked a double. Denny Walling, who'd spent the previous season in the big leagues with the A's, hit a single, then stole second and third, putting himself in perfect scoring position when Dwayne Murphy smacked a double.

The Lookouts nabbed a powerful victory over the Orioles 8-3.

For the rest of the season, Walling played 115 games, scoring 48 times off 95 hits. He earned 42 RBIs, nine homeruns, and carried a .257 batting average. Offensively, he alternated

between third base and outfield. By the end of the season, he was back in Oakland with the Athletics, then spending the remainder of his career through the late 1970s and early 1980s with the Houston Astros.

Murphy, on the other hand, was a late bloomer, coming to Chattanooga after three years with Single A clubs on the West Coast. As a Lookout, in 1976, he scored 32 times off 52 hits, carrying a .260 average. When they sent Murphy to Triple A Tucson for the last half of the season, his average tipped to .235 and he was sent back to Engel Stadium in 1977. For the next season, Murphy played 132 games, scoring 53 times off 104 hits. His average crept back up to .256, enough to call him back to Triple A Vancouver where he stayed on the fast track to the majors. During his 13-year career in the majors, the outfielder found his legs winning the American League Gold Glove Award six times.

The Lookouts' opening day victory set the tone for the rest of the season, with Walling and Murphy at the helm. While the club marched to finish in first place at the end of the first half, the crowd stuck by them.

Through the first three months of play, 65,338 tickets sold and, for the midseason victory, 3,568 watched from the stands. The Lookouts didn't bring home a pennant at the end of the season but the fans didn't care. At the final count, 135,144 turned out through the season to cheer on the team – more than five times the attendance of the Lookouts' final season of play in 1965.

Second only to Montgomery after a one-game championship decided the pennant, Reid swelled with pride. Southern League President Billy Hitchcock credited Chattanooga's return to baseball as the reason the League set an all-time attendance high at more than half a million.

"The people in Chattanooga have really gotten behind their ball club and it looks like they'll draw about 135,000 to lead the League," he said.

Both the Southern League and the minor league praised Reid for bringing baseball back, awarding him two honors for League Executive of the Year.

Reid set a tone at the park that empowered his staff to push the envelope.

During a game on May 17, 1976, Timmons decided to take action from the organist booth against an umpire making a string of bad calls. After waiting for the next obviously bad call, Timmons whooped down on the organ, playing 'Three Blind Mice.'

Angry, the umpire turned red-faced to the press box and shouted, "Stop that music or I'll forfeit the game!"

"Immediately, we called Billy Hitchcock, the president of the league to see if there was anything on the rules allowing an umpire to control what the organist played," Timmons recalled.

When Hitchcock couldn't find anything on the books either way, Timmons and Reid appealed to the commissioner of the Minor League, who stated the umpires had control over the events on the field only, not the entire park. Eager to celebrate the news, Timmons played 'Rock-a-bye, Baby,' which drew a standing ovation.

"The police had to escort the umpire off the field and the story made national news," Timmons said. "It was written up in 'The Sporting News'. The umpires made it an issue during their strike in 1981, demanding they have control over the entire park."

Timmons' witty tune left the young firefighter looking over his shoulder that night. When the police officer on duty at the park jokingly told Timmons he better look out because the umpire was looking for him, Timmons laughingly shrugged it off.

He strode to the lot, got into his 1956 Chrysler New Yorker, and drove straight to his favorite burger joint – Leonard's. While waiting for his burger, a softball umpire strolled through the front door still dressed in his game blue.

"The server, Herbie, said, 'Hey, Charlie! Look!'," Timmons recalled. "I saw that umpire coming through the front door and I *made* a back door. I was certain he'd followed me and was coming to settle the score. I drove so fast that, when I hit a bump, I broke the shocks on my car."

In the spring of 1977, Chattanoogans kept the momentum alive, turning out 7,746 fans to the opening game of the season. The crowd led the league in opening day attendance, giving Chattanooga the coveted Southern League President's Trophy – an award Engel claimed 28 of his 35 years at the helm of the team.

Timmons made a change of his own that would serve to become his trademark.

Irritated with the hum that the florescent lights in the room caused in the speakers, Timmons found a deal on a five-tier chandelier and bought it. After installing the fancy lamp, along with a dimmer switch so he could have a better view of the field, the humming disappeared but the trademark stuck.

"It didn't start out that way but it became my trademark," he said. "It was really an impressive sight to see from East Third Street as you came over the railroad bridge."

The Lookouts, missing Walling but still with Murphy on the field, defended their spot in second place. Despite strong play, attendance slumped to 92,601 for the year. The highlight of the season came at the All-Star break, when homerun legend Hank Aaron came to town with the Atlanta Braves to play the Southern League All-Stars July 7th.

The presence of yet another future hall-of-famer at

A fan looks on as baseball returns to Chattanooga.

Engel Stadium, and a second place finish for the second consecutive year by the Lookouts, was not enough to overcome trouble in the front office, causing the club to tumble into a tailspin.

Engel Stadium Corporation vice president Jim Crittenden told reporters in mid-season he was leaving the franchise. He sold his shares to Reid, claiming the owner didn't discuss financial decisions with him anymore and was taking the Lookouts in a direction he couldn't support.

To make matters worse, Oakland failed for the second consecutive year to deliver on a promise to play an exhibition game against Chattanooga. Reid started hunting for a new affiliate. The change would be the first of many stumbles for the Lookouts to face following their triumphant return to Chattanooga.

Chapter Twenty Two

Power Plays, Pennies, and Politics

On the heels of Oakland's departure from the banks of the Tennessee River, Woody Reid inked a two-year contract with the Cleveland Indians.

Eager to ditch their last place, Double-A affiliate in Jersey City, New Jersey, Cleveland came to Chattanooga in 1978. They seemed to bring poor play with them.

Weeks after the season ended, Crittenden returned to Engel Stadium, buying 60 percent ownership in the Lookouts and making Reid a minority partner, holding just 30 percent of the stock.

The club took the field with Jimmy Bragan as the manager, losing their opening day game against the Knoxville Smokies in front of 5,066 fans. A few strong players came to Chattanooga, such as Joe Charboneau and Sal Rende, but the majority of the players lacked any big league potential.

As the team nose-dived from second place to fifth, fans dispersed and ticket sales plummeted.

Sports reporters were fearful that slumping ticket sales would resort in another affiliate lost and another club disbanded at Engel Stadium. With the pain of an empty stadium still lingering in his mind, Chattanooga Times sports columnist Bill Casteel pleaded to the community to continue supporting the club.

"Attendance is sagging as the Lookouts continue to lose and drop deeper into the cellar," he wrote. "That's the fault of the fans. Give 'em a chance. If they're bad, just chuckle. If they're great, just cheer. After all, there are worse things than a misjudged pop-up or a wild throw to first base. Things like not having a professional baseball team in town."

Casteel's plea went virtually unnoticed and the season's attendance peaked at 53,917 – the lowest since the Lookouts' dismal final year under Engel in 1965.

The faithful fans that did turn out week after week saw first baseman Sal Rende come to town.

In 1978, Rende played 142 games for Chattanooga after spending just one year in the minors. He scored 54 times off 139 hits from 509 at bats and slugged 15 homeruns. Through the course of the next four years as a Lookout, Rende launched a team-record 87 homeruns out of Engel Stadium.

It wouldn't be the last time Rende would reign in Chattanooga.

Aside from Rende's heroics on the field, the rest of the Lookouts faded and fans stopped coming to the park. As ticket sales plunged, profits followed. Reid struggled to maintain the aging stadium and cover his operating costs. To keep the franchise afloat, he took out more loans piling the original $150,000 debt to more than $200,000.

As tensions mounted in the front office, play continued with the Indians new affiliate. On July 30th, 1978, the Lookouts played the longest night game in team history. After five hours thirty-two minutes, and 21 innings of play, the Lookouts defeated Savannah 3-2, just two minutes after the clock struck 1:00 a.m.

After ending the first half of the season in 5th place, the club rallied to finish third, missing a playoff berth for the first time since their return to Engel Stadium.

Only a handful of weeks after the season ended, Reid pulled out of the company completely, citing health reasons, and selling his remaining shares in the franchise to Crittenden.

In his absence, the man who brought Lookouts baseball back to Chattanooga left a $217,000 debt for the new owner to juggle. In an interview a few years later, Reid said personally financing the renovation of the stadium was a mistake that put the club in a deficit that was seemingly impossible to escape.

Still, the community was optimistic Crittenden could turn the club's financials around and secure the future of Lookouts baseball.

As a former member of Joe Engel's Knothole Gang at Bess T. Shepherd School, Crittenden stated publicly that he had a personal interest in restoring the family atmosphere of the Engel era to the ballpark. As a teenager, he was an apprentice of Engel's, selling Cokes and peanuts in the stands during the games.

"I'm sure that being around Engel created a desire of some sort in me to be in his position," Crittenden told the newspaper in 1980. "I greatly admired him and was in awe of him, much more than I was the mayor or governor."

Crittenden quickly cut expenses at the park to counter the mounting debt, firing Charlie Timmons and selling the organ to pay the light bill, according to Timmons.

Under new management, Crittenden and his staff doubled attendance at the park the following year as

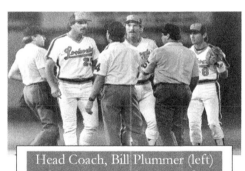

Head Coach, Bill Plummer (left) and two other Lookouts confront the umps on the field.

Charboneau and Rende set single game homerun records, each slugging three, and the Lookouts set a season homerun record of 120 team bombs. At the end of the 1980 season, with attendance now up to 132,338 for the year, Crittenden successfully covered the club's operating expenses but failed to make any headway on his inherited debt.

Desperate, he turned his sights on selling the franchise.

"We've never been able to overcome the deficit we started with," he said. "We can't operate in the red year-in and year-out. Pretty soon it becomes a mental burden."

A Birmingham investor offered to buy the club for a price well below the competitive retail value of a Southern League franchise and Crittenden passed. Instead, he approached the city council and county commissioners for $40,000 – enough to cover his annual expenses for stadium maintenance, insurance, utilities, and grounds keeping – so he could apply his profits to the debt.

His requests were denied.

City council members claimed the ball team didn't draw enough public support to warrant spending public funds to maintain it. County commissioners said no, referencing a recent decision to re-negotiate the lease on the stadium to fund new lights for the field at a price tag of $50,000.

Without a professional buyer or public funding, Crittenden opted for a third route. He brought in a partner, selling 40 percent of the club to Harry Landreth.

The 1981 season fared only slightly better as Kevin Rhomberg led the Southern League with the highest batting average and 149,017 fans came out to watch – the largest season crowd at Engel since the club returned. But when the largest crowd in more than half a decade still wasn't enough to put a dent in the franchise's mountain of debt, a discouraged Crittenden threw in the towel.

"Crittenden came to me and said he was tired of working the baseball circuit," Landreth told reporters, "and that he just wanted to enjoy baseball now."

Despite his financial battles, Crittenden left the Lookouts on firmer financial footing than that which the club started on in 1976 and attendance was rising an average of nearly 30 percent each year.

Crittenden sold his shares to Landreth, who set his sights on improving the quality of play on the field. For four seasons with Cleveland, the Lookouts hovered around fourth place – a fact Landreth attributed to Cleveland's unwillingness to send top-notch players to Chattanooga. As the Lookouts slipped to fifth place by the end of the 1982 season, in front of an annual crowd of 157,948, Landreth bagged a new affiliate for the club.

At the start of the 1983 season, the Lookouts traded in the orange and brown uniforms of the Indians and donned blue and gold as they welcomed the Seattle Mariners to town – the club's fifth major league affiliate to come to the Scenic City in more than a century of organized baseball.

The arrival of the Lookouts' new manager, "Mickey" Bowers was also monumental. Bowers was the first African-American to manage the club.

MARK LANGSTON
Pitcher

"This organization has a lot of pride – Mariner Pride is what it's usually called," Bowers said. "Our owner is a firm believer in raising our players from our own system. Basically, I think that's the right way to do it."

Bowers' career with the Lookouts didn't lost much more than a blink. He was demoted in mid-season for an infraction that happened during spring training in 1982, and was forced into a scouting position with the club.

Mariners' Assistant Farm Director Bill Haywood took his place.

Regardless of the captain, the Mariners new farm team came to Chattanooga to play. Future major league greats, Alvin Davis and Mark Langston led the team from fifth place to third in a single season.

175

On the mound, Langston was a star in Chattanooga. Of the 23 games he started, he won 14 and posted a 3.59 ERA at just 22 years of age. Along with his great successes as a Lookout came a record-setting failure as Langston allowed the most walks in a season – 102 batters! However, Langston's greatness surmounted as he went on to spend 16 years in the majors, winning the American League Gold Glove Award seven times and playing in three All-Star games. In 1988, while with Seattle, he pitched 34 consecutive scoreless innings. Despite his outstanding career, he saw the playoffs only once – in 1998 with the San Diego Padres.

While Langston threw heat from the mound, Alvin Davis stood resolutely by at first base. This rising star also spent only a single season in Chattanooga, hitting 24 doubles, 18 homeruns, 83 RBIs, and toting an on-base percentage of .450! Feared at the bat, Davis set a club record as he was walked 120 times in a season. At the start of the 1984 season, he burst into the majors in Seattle as the American League's Rookie of the Year. He scored 80 of 161 times at bat and drove in 116 RBIs, 27 homeruns, and earned a spot at the All-Star game in his rookie season.

ALVIN DAVIS
Infield

Though his career leveled out in later years, he put on quite a show in Chattanooga and Seattle in the mid-1980s.

Most eyes were on the field in 1983, finally taking attention off the instability in the front office. But the instability was far from gone.

Crittenden filed a civil law suit at the end of the season against Landreth, claiming the new owner had yet to pay for the shares of the club Crittenden sold him at the end of 1982.

The allegation opened a floodgate of claims Landreth was mismanaging funds. City and county officials claimed Landreth owed delinquent taxes. Southern League President, and former Lookouts manager, Jimmy Bragan accused Landreth of falling two months behind on paying the club's league dues. Members of Landreth's own staff also claimed he frequently selected which bills he'd write checks for and which ones he'd let slide by.

Public confidence in the franchise faltered and, while play remained consistent through 1984 under future Mariners head coach Bill Plummer, fan attendance dropped by 20 percent – from 150,000 to 130,000.

Feeling the pressure mounting, Landreth decided to sell the club to Canadian investor, Bill Yuill, in the middle of the 1984 season.

The change seemed to bring a sigh of relief throughout the Southern League.

"We've just got to find out who Bill Yuill is," said Birmingham Barons owner Art Clarkson. "We don't want to go form the frying pan to the fire, and Harry Landreth was definitely the frying pan."

It so happened that the Canadian from Alberta made baseball his business, already owning clubs in Florence, South Carolina and Tucson, Arizona.

"We felt like the challenge in Chattanooga was pretty attractive," Yuill said. "There's not much point in taking over an operation that's perfect. It's tough to improve on that. We kind of have fun improving on an existing situation."

But Yuill was only willing to take on a certain level of challenge. As a condition of the sale, Landreth had to settle all his debts before Yuill took ownership of the club. He likened buying a ball club with debts to a batter stepping to the plate at the bottom of the ninth inning with the bases loaded, two outs and already two strikes showing on the scoreboard.

Bill Yuill's ownership would bring to town another Bill who would come to restore the experience of Lookouts baseball to Chattanooga.

Chapter Twenty Three

"Lee-ave" it to Bill

Yuill became the first absentee owner of the Chattanooga Lookouts – choosing to keep living in his home in Canada rather than move to the Scenic City.

Without the ability to put in the face time required for good customer service and public relations, Yuill knew it was absolutely necessary to pick an outstanding general manager to be the point man for the club. Unsure of who to pick for the job, he went straight to Jimmy Bragan.

Instantly, Bragan knew the perfect man for the job – the man who could make the Lookouts appealing once again to Chattanooga. He told Yuill to call on the Birmingham Barons Assistant General Manager Bill Lee.

For a handful of years in the early 1980s, Lee worked as the Barons public relations manager, then filled the gap as assistant manager. When Yuill came calling for Lee to be the youngest general manager in Double A baseball, Lee was ready to answer. At the start of the 1985 season, Lee came to Engel Stadium.

Lee

"It was very difficult at first," Lee said. "Before we took over, no one gave away tickets and Chattanooga had a history of giving away freebies. We did some good stuff and some new things with radio – things that had been neglected and we made them right."

Yuill brought Jacksonville Suns' broadcaster Larry Ward to town as the Lookouts began live road game broadcasts for the first time in their history.

Along with a new voice on the air waves, fans got a new look on the field as Lee and his staff created Pop-Up – a blue and gold character with a bold mustache, bearing similarities to the Philadelphia Phillies' mascot- The Phanatic.

A new voice and new mascot still wasn't enough. Lee set his eyes on the empty organ booth, knowing the stadium needed that old familiar sound to excite the crowd. Lee budgeted $50 per game to pay Charlie Timmons to play, then called Timmons to talk.

"I brought him in and asked what it would take for him to play the organ at the games again," Lee said. "He sighed and thought about it, then said he had to have $25 per game. I looked at him and said that was a tough request. He said he'd totally re-do the organ booth and the sound system. To this day, he has no idea I was willing to pay him $50."

Timmons surely doesn't mind.

"Bill led the absolute best years of Lookouts baseball," Timmons said. "He was a real people person."

Finally, before the season started, Lee decided to have a party. The 1985 season marked the 100th anniversary of the Lookouts' affiliation with the Southern League. They sold commemorative edition Louisville Slugger bats, pennants, baseballs, and even put up billboards around town inviting the community to celebrate at the ballpark.

"On the first night of the 1985 season, we had it all planned out," Lee said. "It was going to be great. It was all scripted with the fireworks planned. You name it, we had it. I told the pyrotechnic guy to set off a single firework during the National Anthem, when they sing, '…the bombs bursting in air…'."

The Lookouts took the field and the crowd grew silent as the game opened with an invocation. Before the invocation finished, the fireworks started.

"I was standing halfway down the first base line during the middle of the invocation when I heard a boom," Lee said. "Then I heard another."

By accident, even before the National Anthem began, the technician set off the entire fireworks display.

"I was screaming bloody murder down the first base line," he said.

"Through the season, Lee introduced promotions like Aunt Jemima Nights – featuring the famous maiden of maple syrup manufactured in Chattanooga. Another promotion ran throughout the season, outfitting children with complete Lookouts uniforms – hats, jerseys, gloves, and wristbands – requiring each wide-eyed child to come to the park to collect all four! Adult fans were entertained by the grocery dashes, when fans were pitted against each other with grocery carts and raced around the base lines for prizes.

"A Winner Never Quits"
In 1985, film crews shot A Winner Never Quits in Chattanooga, featuring Engel Stadium prominently. Keith Carradine – the star of nearly forty feature films and more than twenty cable and network television movies – starred as Pete Gray, a one-armed player for the St. Louis Browns.

"We all thought we'd get a chance to be in the movie," said former general manager Bill Lee. "We taught Carradine how to bat left handed. All our stuff wound up on the cutting room floor."

Engel Stadium was the setting of another movie in 1999 – All Over Again. Robert Loggia and Craig T. Nelson starred in a story about a man who had an opportunity to travel back in time and change how his life would turn out.

Despite the changes, fans were skeptical of the club after Landreth's financial debacle and attendance plummeted to 112,700 as the club finished in fifth place.

But Lee was in it for the long haul, keeping his eyes on the steady attendance increase as play improved and the atmosphere at the park took a turn for the better.

When play resumed in 1986, the Lookouts sat firmly in fifth place but he made some changes in his staff.

"On the second game of the 1986 season, we got rain," Lee said. "While we were pulling the tarp over the field, I was yelling and cussing because that's what you do when you're a first-time general manager – you scream your head off because you have no control over yourself.

"My head groundskeeper told me that I didn't need to cuss so much. I told him I'd *?#! cuss if I wanted to *?#! cuss and if he didn't like it he could get off my *?#! field!"

The groundskeeper's next reaction surprised Lee.

"He walked off the field right then," he said. "So I pointed to Tony Inzer, who was standing by the dugout, and said, 'You're me new head groundskeeper.' He said he didn't know anything about grounds keeping and I told him I didn't care, just the grab the tarp. He stayed with me for four years."

Timmons remembered Inzer as having missed his calling by becoming a groundskeeper.

Tony looked like a bull, boy, was he built," Timmons said. "After the games, they'd have batting practice and Tony would comfortably hit balls out of the park in right center – 330 to 340 feet."

Lee agreed, saying, "I should have hired Tony as my manager but instead I made him my groundskeeper. That shows what a great judge of talent I am."

Regardless of whether Lee could judge talent, he was willing to help people be happy.

When minority owner Carrington Montague came around the park looking for something to do, Lee had to answer honestly.

"He was so desperate to do something at the park and to have a desk but I didn't have anything for him to do," Lee said. "Finally, I gave him a desk and assigned him to the task of changing all the calendars at the start of every month. He said, 'I'll do it.' On the first business day of every month, he was there!"

Even the Coca-Cola vendor was comfortable around Lee, stopping frequently at Engel Stadium simply to use Lee's restroom.

The season ended with the club in fifth place and attendance notching up about 8,000 fans.

Certain better play on the field would fill the seats around it, Yuill and Lee called a familiar face back to Engel Stadium to try to turn the team around.

In 1982, Sal Rende left the Lookouts having set a handful of records, including the career homerun record. By 1984, he landed in Appleton, Wisconsin, where he managed the Foxes to the league championships and earned the title of manager of the year. The next season, he again led the team to the best record in the league and, in 1986, he led Seattle's farm club in Bellingham, Washington to a pennant win in the Northwest League – Rende's second pennant win in three years.

Seattle took notice and, when Yuill and Lee wanted to turn things around on the field, everyone agreed Rende was the man for the job, carrying a career win-loss record of 217-132.

Though Rende coached in the Northwest, he and his wife, Toni, held an off-season home in Chattanooga since 1981. He was eager to accept the job.

"I'm really happy at the chance to manage here," he told the News Free Press in December 1986. "This was something I'd sort of had in the back of my mind since I joined the Seattle organization. I guess you could say I had a say in my coming here because I could have joined another organization."

On the field, Rende was strict on pitchers, not one to loosely call for an intentional walk. He was tight on hitters too, rarely calling for sacrifice bunts from his batters, more interested in seeing his boys at the plate swing for the ball. Certainly, the Lookouts' homerun leader preferred batters to swing rather than stand idly by or take lame chops at a pitch.

Rende's prowess at the plate stayed with him in his years as coach. Lee recalled many nights when he and Rende would face off hitting homeruns at Engel Stadium. The winner of the two-man derby won a Dairy Queen Blizzard, compliments of the loser.

"I bought him a lot of Blizzards," Lee said. "I think he bought me one."

Through 143 games, the Lookouts won 68 and lost 75, bringing Rende his first losing season as a head coach and cementing their spot in fourth place. Rende predicted it would take at least two seasons for Seattle's Single A talent to reach Double A Chattanooga, but that day would never come.

By the end of the season, Bill Yuill got an itch to sell the middle-of-the-pack Lookouts, drawing little more than 115,000 fans each year. Seattle was quickly losing interest as well.

Rumors of yet another affiliate change abounded – potentially, the Lookouts' fourth parent club in about a decade.

Rende left at the end of the season to manage the Royals farm club in Memphis. Seattle pulled their affiliation with the Lookouts and Yuill turned his sights to the Northwest. Yuill bolted to Seattle to start a new venture owning a minor league hockey team at the edge of the Puget Sound. He sold the Lookouts to Chicago real estate developer, Rick Holtzman, then asked Lee to go with him.

"It wasn't the right time for me," Lee said. "I felt like I still had things to do in Chattanooga."

Before Yuill left, he inked a deal with the Cincinnati Reds to become the new affiliate of the Lookouts.

Newspapers touted the change as Chattanooga obtaining the Cadillac of ball clubs. The Scenic City was also eager to see

Holtzman. The Chicago native owned two ball teams – one in Davenport, Iowa, and another in Midland, Texas – and lived just two blocks away from Wrigley Field. He picked up the Lookouts for $1.2 million and became Chattanooga's fifth owner in twelve years.

The Scenic City ball team was on the brink of greatness or obscurity – suffering wavering attendance and mediocre play – as they embarked on yet another chapter at Engel Stadium.

This chapter would be the greatest yet.

"The Real Thing"
Two large, concrete Coca-Cola bottles used to sit on the centerfield wall at Engel Stadium. If a player ever hit the bottles with a ball, it counted as an automatic homerun and the player got $1,000!

Chapter Twenty Four

Happy Days are Here Again

At the start of the 1988 season, Engel Stadium had stood at the corner of East Third and O'Neal for nearly 60 years.

Babies born in Chattanooga when the stands went up now bounced grandchildren on their knees. The stadium's namesake had lain in the Forest Hills Cemetery for nearly 20 years and the stadium itself stood practically vacant for a decade.

It was starting to show its age.

When Holtzman came to Chattanooga to survey his purchase, he instantly knew this club could not call this house a home. The oldest ballpark in Minor League Baseball still in use was held together by patchwork meant to stop the spreading hand of time in this corner or that. Holtzman saw the Band-Aids no longer healed the broken bones beneath. Something had to be done.

In March, the new owner went to the city council and the county commission with a simple message: Renovate Engel Stadium, to the tune of $2 million, or I'm leaving Chattanooga and taking my baseball team with me.

Holtzman's proposal would have made Engel one of the nicest parks in the country, complete with air-conditioned suites, elevators, and other extravagant extras – all things government officials and the general public frowned upon.

"They smack of elitism and are not in keeping with the historic character of the stadium," read one Times editorial.

But the problems were real.

The stadium's clubhouses were in such disrepair, some visiting teams refused to change in them, instead opting to dress at the hotel before getting on the bus to the park. Old concessions booths caused long lines and longer waits and sparse bathrooms often ran out of supplies when the park dew a large crowd.

The city and the county had a lot to think about; neither having been approached by Yuill for anything during his tenure.

"The seventh-inning stretch is over," said commissioner Paul Nolan. "We're back in there pitching again."

On the field, the Lookouts started the season under a new coach, Tom Runnels. He snapped the players into shape and the club finished the first half of the season in first place.

"This was one of the most close-knit, unusual teams in my history," Timmons said. "They had extreme self-discipline. Most players would party, sleep half the day, and then come play the game. Tom had the team practicing at 10 a.m., 2 p.m., then they'd play the game. It was a regular routine."

The work ethic of one bled over into the work ethic of all.

"I couldn't tell you how many locker room brawls took place," Timmons said. "If one guy wasn't putting out 100 percent, that army would go after that one not pulling his load. The majority went on to play in the majors and that's the big reason why."

Bill Lee knew exactly why the 1988 club was so good.

"Branch Rickey, III, was the farm director for the Reds in 1987," he said. "He let me come down and select our ball club. I told him I've got to

> "Schott"
>
> "The only time I met Marge Schott was at the winter meeting in December of 1987," said former general manager Bill Lee. "I introduced myself and she asked, 'Do you like dogs?' I said I had Samoyeds, and she said, 'Then you must be alright then.'"

have at least one bomber, a left-handed bomber, three mountain goats in the outfield and some vacuum cleaners in the infield."

The club was on track to draw the largest crowed to the park in five seasons while the Lookouts pursued championship dreams. City and county officials were not ignorant of the magic happening at Engel Stadium and, in July, both bodies budgeted a combined total $1.5 million to renovate the aging ballpark. Each stated they were willing to finance additional projects in the future as deemed necessary.

Though Holtzman couldn't claim an outright victory, he was pleased with the results and he watched the team play out the rest of their season.

Through the first half of the season, the Lookouts won 43 of 73 games before hearing the news their home would be restored. After the All-Star break, the team kept their noses to the grindstone, winning 38 of 70 games and heading to the Southern League championship series for the first time since 1976.

From the mound, the Lookouts pursued the pennant with passion. Keith Brown and Chris Hammond carried ERA's of 1.42 and 1.72 respectively, both winning a combined 25 of 31 starts. Scott Scudder posted a 2.96 ERA, winning all of his seven starts. The club also had depth, relying on Mike Smith and Mike Roesler to pitch consistently and render the opposing offense useless.

Infielder Keith Lockhart scored once of every two times he hit through the season, carrying an average of .266. Outfielder Chris Jones remained as steady, scoring 50 times off 111 hits.

While catcher Joe Oliver and major league veteran Ron Oester only spent a short time in Chattanooga during the season, both made significant contributions to the team's success.

Through 14 games, Oester carried a .304 average while Oliver followed suit swinging .248, scoring 9 of 26 hits.

On September 12th, the Lookouts met on the field to face the Greenville, Mississippi Braves.

"On the day of that playoff game, I sensed the electricity in that crowd," Timmons said. "As I walked in the front gate and went to my post, the hair rose up on the back of my neck and I got cold sweats.

"At the start of the first inning, before the first batter took the first swing, I hit the plain old, everyday 'CHARGE' and the place roared. I knew right then and there I was going to be in for a ride and, buddy, I was. I felt the building go up and down from the momentum of the crowd."

The team played as they had all season.

On that September night, in front of a crowd of 2,213, the Lookouts got down to business.

In the first inning, Hedi Vargas hit a grand slam, Jones slapped a two-run triple, and Oliver powered a two-run homer over Third Street. The Lookouts were quickly on top 5-0.

For the next five innings, Smith threw fire from the mound.

"I told them they'd have to take a crowbar to take the ball out of my hands," Smith said. "I was going to pitch a complete game."

Bernie Walker celebrates with teammates after the club's most recent pennant win.

In the third, the Lookouts nabbed three more runs, shaming the Braves sole point in the second. By the sixth inning, the tension between the clubs erupted after Lookout Brian Finley was hit with a pitch. Both benches cleared, Finley received a cut ear, and then was ejected, along with teammate Luis Reyna and Greenville pitcher, Maximo Del Rosario.

When the dust settled, the Lookouts fought back on offense. Lockhart claimed his sixth postseason homerun, setting the stage for the club to claim five more runs in the seventh inning.

The team claimed their first Southern League pennant in 27 years, defeating the Braves 13-2.

"It's always easier to pitch when your team puts 13 runs on the board," Smith said. "That's what it takes, a team effort."

The stadium erupted.

Fans rushed the field as players lifted them onto their shoulders, as remembered in Ken Burns legendary documentary, Baseball.

"The players didn't retreat into the privacy of the clubhouse to celebrate. They hoisted fans ... and paraded them across the diamond, sharing bottles of champagne. In the booth behind home plate, the Hammond organ boomed out 'Happy Days are Here Again.' For thirty minutes, the infield was a swirling mass of raucous celebrants. Said Hedi Vargas; 'This is my first pennant. It will be in my heart always, for the rest of my life.'"

The club loved their fans, voting to give one dedicated ticket holder – Hubert Qarrels – one of the club's championship rings.

The 1988 Lookouts laid the framework for the Reds' 1990 World Series Championship team – including Lockhart, Oester, Oliver, Brown, Hammond, and Scudder. At the end of the 90s, Lockhart joined the Atlanta Braves and helped the club win six division titles, one National League championship, and a shot at a second World Series title in a decade.

It marked the team's seventh pennant victory in 104 years. The milestone would usher in the last great decade at Historic Engel Stadium.

Chapter Twenty Five

Two Million Dead Presidents

The winter of 1988 likely proved to be the most hectic off-season in the history of the team.

"I worked with a great bunch of people," Lee said. "People who really cared like a big family. Then came the renovation. That was hard. We worked out of a trailer and it was just a freakin' mess. We were trying to do things in a real haphazard way."

After winning the Southern League pennant, the team disappeared for the winter and the real work began. Construction crews rolled down East Third Street, facing the daunting task of renovating a 59-year-old monster.

The project drew a $2 million price tag and a short window of opportunity to completely overhaul one of the cities last connections to Depression-era baseball. To boot, crews would later labor in the coldest months of the year to have the park open for play in spring.

Crews worked tirelessly through the holiday season, respecting deadlines and mending walls as opening day rapidly approached.

When March rolled around and crews were still working, tensions started to run high.

"One day in March, during the renovation, it was raining like hell and the pressure was building," Timmons said. "We were all down at the park every day. The carpenters and electricians were standing on Coca-Cola flats under the stadium because the water was running just like a creek.

"Everyone was working so fast that mistakes were being made."

One by one, reports of mistakes came to the anxious Lee, who was working out of a temporary office in a trailer on the property.

Accidentally, crews misread the blueprint and bricked in the doorway to the walk-in cooler.

In the organ booth, electricians wired the 220-watt organ with a 110-watt plug.

Finally, from the window of the trailer office, Timmons spied a painter working on an advertisement, and misspelling the word 'SMIRNOFF.'

"Bill had a temper that would just flash so, when I told him about the painter, he shouted, "What?", said Timmons. "He was already irritated and he was near-sighted, so he just took a quick glance out the window and said, "No, it's right."

Lee's secretary spoke up vouching for Timmons by pointing out the painter's mistake.

"Bill got an umbrella and slammed the door so hard that I thought it would fall off," Timmons said. "He unloaded on that painter."

When Lee got done yelling, he returned to his office seething with frustration and not wanting to talk. Timmons knew someone had to ease the pressure the staff was feeling so he grabbed Tony Inzer and headed to his car.

"I had some scuba gear in my car, so Tony put it on," Timmons said. "Then, wearing the flippers and the mask, he walked into Bill's office and asked him if there was anything else he needed to do that day.

"I'll never forget how hard Bill laughed. It was hilarious."

Despite the setbacks, work continued at Engel Stadium. However, soon it became apparent to everyone the heavy rains had delayed the completion of the project.

With the playing field resurfaced and half a ballpark still under construction, the 1989 season started.

"When

> ## "*Urine* the Wrong Place"
> On August 5th, 2005, WUSY, US 101 FM radio personality "Big Al" recounted a story of one of his most memorable trips to Engel Stadium following the 1989 renovation. As can sometimes happen at the ballpark on a hot day, Big Al needed to make a quick break to the men's restroom after downing a few drinks trying to stay cool.
> "I really had to go so I wasn't paying that much attention. I thought I was going in the men's restroom entrance door, but I really went in the women's restroom exit door!"
> Luckily for Al, he was the only one inside. Unfortunately for Al, he mistakenly took the newly renovated sink (designed in a large, circular 'trough' style) as a "fancy urinal."
> In the midst of his relief, a female friend walked through the door and shouted, "What are you *doing* in here?"
> "I shouted back, 'What are *you* doing in here?' She told me I was in the women's restroom and that I was using the sink! I just thought it was really fancy! I was so embarrassed, all I could think of was getting out of there. It happened so many years ago but I've never been able to live that down."
> Sorry, "Big Al", I fear you never will.

we opened the season, half the stadium wasn't ready but we decided we were going to really dress it up like the grand opening of a movie," Lee said. "All the guys dressed in tuxedos."

Timmons sat in the organ booth, no longer under a five-tier chandelier, but a new ten-tier chandelier.

"I was walking down the third base line in my beautiful black tuxedo I'd rented and everyone was sort of staring at me,"

Lee said. "I felt really good until I realized some kid had run some mustard down the middle of my back like a skunk."

It was a sign of things to come.

Mistakes continued.

The restaurant at the ballpark had no view of the field and, initially, sports reporters couldn't see home plate from the press box.

Engel Stadium with a facelift.

The largest problem came on the field.

After crews resurfaced the playing field and installed a material similar to burlap to help with drainage, the club discovered this field didn't drain. The Lookouts couldn't play 14 games due to rain outs, including the entire 4th of July weekend – traditionally, Minor League Baseball's biggest draw.

The issue spurred Holtzman to file a lawsuit against the city

and county for the mistakes. Two years later, a jury found in favor of the Lookouts and ordered the two governments to pay a combined total $496,720.68 for repairs and damages incurred to the club.

Just one season after their pennant victory, the team slumped to fourth place, losing all of their power players to Triple A Nashville or Cincinnati.

The Lookouts tumbled into fourth place by the All-Star break, then into fifth at the season's end. Still, 156,677 fans came out to see the new park – the largest crowd at Engel since 1982.

During one of those games, Bill Lee took an opportunity to set a new tone at the ballpark – one of family fun and safety rather than beer drinking and rowdiness.

"One night, I saw a guy carrying one of our bats out of the locker room," Lee said. "He was a pretty good size guy and I watched him go back to his seat, around a bunch of Harley-looking guys.

"I approached them and said I saw you steal that bat. He said he didn't and I told him that I saw him do it. Then he said he wanted to talk to the guy in charge. I said that was me. He gave me the bat and I threw him out of the park."

Feeling successful in defending his club against bullies, Lee went about his business, putting the issue out of his mind.

At the end of the game, he assumed his post in front of the ballpark, shaking hands and thanking people for coming to the game as he traditionally did. When he saw a group of ten to fifteen rough-looking guys walking toward him, the events of the evening came rushing back.

"All I could think of was how to get back to my office so I could hide," Lee said. "But someone stopped me. Then the biggest, burliest guy approached me and asked if I was Bill Lee."

"Yes," Lee replied.

"You're the general manager?"

"Yes."

"That was my friend you threw out of here."

"Really?"

Fearful he was about to be pummeled in the parking lot by an angry mob of motorcycle gang members, Lee nervously awaited his fate.

Then he was utterly shocked.

"He said, 'That's the way this park should have been run the whole time. I own [Thunder Creek] Harley Davidson here in town and I want to talk to you about advertising here next here,'" Lee said. "I just about *#*! myself."

In 1990, attendance sank again as word spread Rick Holtzman filed for personal bankruptcy. Despite telling reporters not to worry, that the Lookouts would not be affected by this reorganization of his personal assets, gun-shy fans avoided the park.

For the year, 141,743 came to the newly restored park – 15,000 less than the previous season.

Matters in the front office weren't faring much better for Lee as the club's finances started to mirror the Landreth years.

"When you have an absentee owner, the general public doesn't know who the owner is so they linked it with me," Lee said. "Holtzman wasn't paying his bills so I'd take the cash from all the concessions at the end of the night and call the folks who didn't get paid that month. I'd tell them, if you want your money, come get it tonight."

Lee claims the issue led to his resignation at the end of the season.

"Holtzman told me if I wasn't going to do things his way, then I should leave," he said. "So I left."

Lee, the general manager who returned family fun to Engel Stadium and a much needed facelift to an aging ballpark, took only good memories with him.

"When people ask me what's my favorite town I've been in, by far it's Chattanooga," said Lee, who now serves as the commissioner of the Frontier League. "The people were the greatest. I know I could go back right now and be made to feel at home. I was made to feel like a celebrity. Some really wonderful stuff happened."

Lee and the championship Lookouts were gone in 1991 and the club faced one of the toughest five-year periods in the history of professional baseball.

An Explosive Day at the Park

In 1991, Pat "Midnight" O'Brien, a.k.a. "Captain Dynamite", was a featured performer at Engel Stadium. Just one more reason to go out to the old ball game – you might catch more than just a foul ball!

Chapter Twenty Six

The Lookouts' New Look

On December 17, 1990, Bill Davidson replaced Bill Lee as the general manager of the Lookouts.

Things in the office turned around as Holtzman brought in a general manager who, according to Timmons, was a "real bean counter. If you want a financials and investments guy, he was your man."

With Davidson watching the numbers and future Los Angeles Dodgers manager Jim Tracy watching the players on the field, the club rebounded into second place, drawing the largest crowd since the Lookouts won the pennant in 1952.

Word spread far and wide that the Lookouts logo – a simple Chicago Bears-style 'C' – was one of the ugliest in professional baseball. Davidson quickly helped design a new logo featuring a block type 'C' donning two cartoon eyeballs. The public was quick to embrace the Lookouts' new look and, clad in the new insignia, the 1992 Lookouts finished first in their division – losing in the playoffs in their attempt to bag an eighth league pennant.

Davidson and Holtzman saw a huge increase in attendance as 269,688 fans followed the club to the playoffs through the season – the largest crowd at Engel Stadium in the history of the park.

The Lookouts' new general manager credited the spike in attendance to the Atlanta Braves outstanding season, wherein the club claimed the first of 14 consecutive division titles. He stated fans that wanted to see a baseball game, but couldn't get to Atlanta, settled instead for a day at Engel Stadium to satisfy their renewed desire for a day at the old ballpark.

Outside factors continued to drive local attendance through the next few years.

In 1992, Marge Schott, the owner of the Lookouts' parent club in Cincinnati, made national headlines when some claimed she referred to two of her players, Eric Davis and Dave Parker, as her "million-dollar niggers." The same accusers claimed she owned an armband donning the Nazi swastika. Defending herself to the New York Times, she said she was not a racist. Two weeks later, she told the Times that Adolf Hitler was initially good for Germany and that she didn't understand why the term "Jap" was so offensive, when referring to a Japanese person.

Major League Baseball appointed a committee to investigate Schott.

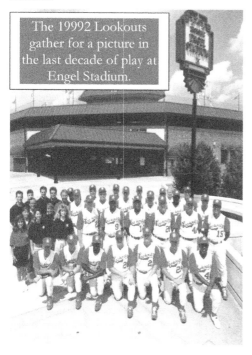

The 19992 Lookouts gather for a picture in the last decade of play at Engel Stadium.

In February 1993, Schott was fined $25,000 and banned from the day-to-day operations of the organization for an entire year.

The Reds came to Chattanooga on April 19th to play an exhibition game with the Lookouts as Cincinnati's home office tried to mend fences. Disgruntled fans turned their attention away from the Reds and closer to home, and churned out yet another record crowd at Engel Stadium as the club finished in second place.

The following year drew the largest crowd ever seen at Engel during the 20th century.

In the spring of 1994, the Greater Chattanooga Sports Committee decided fans were desperate to honor the players of years past. They established the Chattanooga Baseball Hall of Fame and inducted eight members at a banquet held at the Trade Center downtown.

Inductees, Fergie Jenkins and Harmon Killebrew, spoke at the ceremony on their way to Florida to participate in the annual Old Timers game. Along with Jenkins and Killebrew, Chattanooga inducted Kiki Cuyler, Rogers Hornsby, Joe Engel, Clark Griffith, Burleigh Grimes, and Satchel Paige.

Through the season, fans didn't turn out to see legendary Lookouts, instead filling the stands to see a Michael "Air" Jordan.

The hall-of-fame Chicago Bulls guard and twelve-time NBA All-Star, who won three NBA championships in 1991, 1992, and 1993, spent a single season – 1994 – pursuing a career in Minor League Baseball as an outfielder for the Birmingham Barons, the Double A farm club for the Chicago White Sox.

Batting and throwing right, Jordan played 127 games stepping to the plate 436 times. He scored 46 times off 88 hits – 17 doubles, one triple, three homeruns, and 51 RBIs posting a .202 batting average. Jordan battled the Lookouts in Chattanooga three times that season bringing with him the largest crowds since the Lookouts were part of the Southern Association in the 1950s.

"Cheap Seats" Legendary country music group, Alabama, recorded the music video to their gold selling single, 'Cheap Seats', at Engel Stadium during a Lookouts game in 1993.

On his first trip, 14,137 packed the 10,000-seat Engel Stadium. Jordan's second trip attracted 13,416 fans while a third trip that season drew 9,827 to the park to see the slam dunk champion take a swing at a career in baseball. Despite his best efforts, Jordan couldn't make a career out of baseball, retiring in March 1995. He returned to the NBA and won three more NBA championships before retiring again in 1998 – then playing two more seasons with the Washington Wizards in 2001 and 2002.

As the Lookouts charged back in the second half of the season from fifth place to finish first in their division, talk of a strike in Major League Baseball abounded. Players argued that owners weren't sharing enough of the money they made and, unable to reach a compromise, walked out of the last three months of the 1994 season in mid-August.

Most fans weren't sympathetic.

"It's ridiculous," one Baltimore locksmith told ESPN. "Most of the players make over $1 million a year. School teachers make it on $30,000. What do they have to complain about? I'm not paying to watch million-dollar cry babies."

Instead, fans kept their attention at the local level watching hungry young men play for meager wages and lots of sacrifice to chase a dream and play a game. While major league parks across the country sat alone in the dark, 292,920 fans cheered the Lookouts for their desire to play for the love of the game.

At the end of the 1994 season, Holtzman faced a hard truth.

Record setting attendance at Engel Stadium was doing nothing more than keeping pace with the rising cost of maintaining the 65-year-old park. From 1990 to 1994, the estimated cost of running the club, spiked by $150,000 – from $250,000 to $396,000.

Holtzman decided it was a price he was no longer willing to pay. At the end of the year, he found a buyer for the club.

A man named Frank – a businessman from Maine – fell in love with Engel Stadium and quickly purchased the Lookouts for a price somewhere between $3.5 to $4 million – almost four times his purchase price of $1.2 million in 1987.

The man from Maine would bring the legacy of the Joe Engel-era Lookouts full circle, drawing record crowds to the park with some of the most innovative promotions in Minor League Baseball.

Cheering the Lookouts

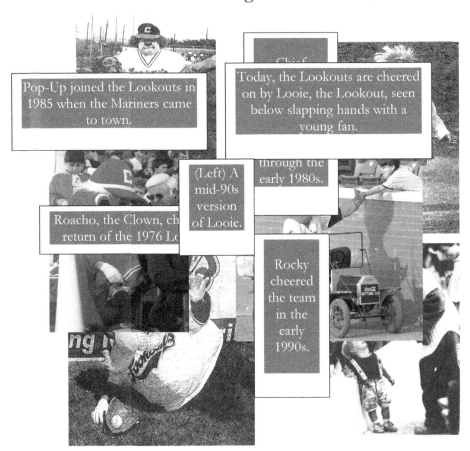

Pop-Up joined the Lookouts in 1985 when the Mariners came to town.

Today, the Lookouts are cheered on by Looie, the Lookout, seen below slapping hands with a young fan.

through the early 1980s.

(Left) A mid-90s version of Looie.

Roacho, the Clown, ch return of the 1976 L

Rocky cheered the team in the early 1990s.

Chapter Twenty Seven

The Maine Difference

Like Joe Engel, whose father owned a string of hotels and brother was an executive at RCA, Frank Burke was part of an entrepreneurial legacy.

Burke's father, Daniel, retried from Capital Cities, Inc., after orchestrating the purchase of the American Broadcasting Company – more commonly known as ABC. His older brother, Steve, now serves as the chief operating officer at Comcast, after working for many years running EuroDisney and successfully launching The Disney Store in shopping malls across the nation. Burke's younger brother, Bill, was the president of WTBS, the chief executive officer of The Weather Channel, and successfully chartered the maiden voyage of Turner Classic Movies onto the open cable airwaves. He now lives in Maine, where he is writing the autobiography of Ted Turner. Uncle James Burke was the chairman at Johnson and Johnson before retiring in the early 1990s then ran the Partnership for a Drug Free America until 2002.

"There are days I wish I was making the money they make," Frank said. "But there are days when my brothers wish they did what I do."

The new Lookouts owner was no slouch, having earned a bachelor's degree in Political Science from Middlebury College and an MBA from Harvard Business School. After working as a production assistant at ABC's Wide

World of Sports, then owning an AM/FM radio chain in Maine, Burke decided to buy the Lookouts.

Burke's father owned the Portland Sea Dogs, the Double-A affiliate of the Boston Red Sox, and Frank helped out around the club along with general manager, Charles Eshbach.

After looking around and weighing their options, the three men pinpointed Chattanooga as the place to leave their next mark on the national pastime.

"Finding Engel Stadium was a bit like falling in love," Burke said. "Initially, you don't see some of the downsides. We saw a great place to watch a ballgame. There's a lot of value in Double-A baseball in Chattanooga, and we thought we could overcome some of the obstacles. The Lookouts have been here so long, we thought they'd been taken for granted."

In the winter of 1994, the man from Maine moved with his wife and three children to Chattanooga.

"There's no substitute for local ownership," he said. "You can't exist without a sense of ownership by the community."

In his first years at the park, the Lookouts battled for yet another pennant, finishing first in their division in front of a crowd of 290,002. It marked the first time a change in ownership didn't cause a substantial slump in attendance since the club's return in 1976.

"Come One, Come All"

One of Burke's most prized accomplishments was fairly simple.

When he learned a small gate at the edge of the park along the third base line, at the corner of O'Neal and East Third, used to be the 'colored entrance' before segregation, Burke ordered the gate bricked up.

"It was one of the greatest things I could have done," he said. "I want this park to be open to everyone and we should all walk through the same gates."

Burke's passion for the team was contagious.

"This is the club we wanted," he told reporters in 1995. "In my opinion, it's a historic franchise and it's just a wonderful ballpark. For those who have seen it so many times, maybe it doesn't awe you the way it does us. But there are people spending millions of dollars around the country trying to recreate Engel Stadium in one form or another. It's kind of Camden Yards before there was Camden Yards."

Through his first season, Burke learned the park wasn't completely perfect but was committed to making it that way.

One female fan told him, after a game in front of the park, that the parking lot needed lights, claiming it was too dark and she didn't feel safe.

Burke added lights.

He replaced the old mascot – a raccoon Burke dubbed, "Rocky, the rug sample" – with a new mascot, the Trash Monster.

He painted the stadium, signed a new lease with the county, and improved the sound system.

After all this, he printed the improvements on a card along with a guarantee for two free tickets to any Lookouts baseball game, redeemable for the best seats available in the house.

"Every time someone told me they hadn't been to a game in years, I gave them this card," he said. "No excuses. I'm not worried about how we get things done. You only have one chance to be new."

Likely, it was that very line of thinking that inspired Burke to bring Lumpy and Larry to Engel Stadium at the

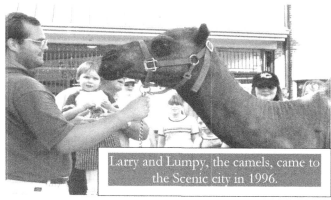

Larry and Lumpy, the camels, came to the Scenic city in 1996.

start of his second season in Chattanooga.

205

"My dad didn't understand it when I brought those two camels to the ballpark," Burke said. "But when he saw them walking across the Third Street bridge from Warner Park as the sun was setting, he told me, 'Now I understand.'"

The camels roamed in the outfield, near the LOOKOUTS sign, in the deepest centerfield in the history of the game.

Above the camels sat Burke's greatest idea – the Chattanooga Choo Choo. Burke built a replica steam engine and sat it on a track at the top of the centerfield wall. Each time the Lookouts hit a homerun or won a game, the train would smoke and ride the short track along the top of the wall.

"I've had people offer me ads to run on the train but I've always said no," he said. "I guess there are some things that are just mine."

With camels grazing in the outfield, the Lookouts again returned to the top of the League and competed for the pennant, but to no avail. However, flooding on the field and electrical issues at the aging ballpark drove fans away as attendance dipped to 227,885 – the smallest crowd since 1991.

Burke refused to give up on the park, instead looking for another promotion to draw a crowd.

At the start of the 1997 season, he sent the camels packing to nearby Warner Park Zoo, trading the desert mammals for Louise, the Lookouts Fan. Louise had a single job – to deliver the baseballs to the umpire during the game.

But there was a twist.

Instead of a camel, Louise was a pregnant donkey.

That spring, at the start of the 1997 season, the owner of the Chattanooga Times Free Press started to talk about the white elephant in the Scenic City's living room – the aging Engel Stadium.

Roy Exum penned an open letter to newly-elected city mayor John Kinsey, lobbying on behalf of the Lookouts and the city for a new baseball stadium.

"Frank Burke is a sunny and personable guy who has made a Sunday afternoon at the ballpark into a good and wholesome thing," he wrote. "But the awful fact is that Engel Stadium is falling down."

To that point, no one had ever suggested replacing Engel Stadium – the historic home to baseball's legends, legacies, and most eccentric owner in the game, comparable only to zany White Sox owner, Bill Veeck.

Exum said the stadium not only hurt the Lookouts but Chattanooga's opportunity to host other tourist draws. When he approached the Southeastern Conference about hosting their collegiate baseball tournament in Chattanooga, the conference said the stadium was "inadequate."

Some Chattanoogans supported the idea while others fought to calm the bristling hairs on their necks over the mere mention of moving Lookouts baseball off the corner of East Third, where it had been since 1909.

Burke held his tongue.

The Lookouts drew 228,391 fans to the park as the club finished the season in third place – the first time the club didn't make the divisional playoffs since Burke took over. At the end of the season, Burke spoke publicly about his problems at Engel Stadium for the first time.

Nearly every time the rain fell, the field flooded, canceling games and costing tickets. The concessions and clubhouse areas were deemed barely hospitable by the Southeastern Conference and electrical issues continued to plague the park. Finally, at the start of every season – 1995, 1996, and 1997 – Burke paid $12,000 to paint the wooden bleachers now rotting away after years of weather.

"Engel Stadium is an unbelievable place to try to maintain," Burke told reporters. "Seventy percent of our operating expenses go to fixing things."

207

Still not willing to give up on the park, dedicated to making repairs that might save the stadium, Burke bid on a new sound system. To his surprise, his $10,000 bid won the entire sound system from the Atlanta Braves former home – Fulton County Stadium – estimated to be worth $200,000. The entire set – numbering more than a dozen speakers – came to Chattanooga with some being used at Engel and others at the softball fields at Warner Park. Still a few remained.

"I may put one on my car and crank up a Deep Purple tape," Burke joked.

When the park opened in 1998, the club was in fifth place. By midseason, it was evident the problems that plagued the park weren't going to go away.

Despite the neighbors outstanding support of the franchise, Burke's office was broken into three times, costing him a laptop

Renovations in 1989 weren't enough to solve all of Engel's problems.

each time. The park was also about five miles away from the nearest interstate off-ramp and about the same distance from the re-emerging vibrancy in downtown Chattanooga. Finally, structural repairs needed at the park started to rival the cost of building a brand new stadium.

In July 1998, Burke told city and county officials that he needed a new home for his ball team, or he'd be forced to cut his losses and sell the club.

The city and county turned an unsympathetic ear to his request, stating they simply didn't have the funds to build a new stadium in the Scenic City.

Times Free Press columnist Chris Dortch penned this response to Burke's request, printed July 24th, 1998:

"Realistically speaking, the Lookouts, or any Chattanooga franchise, would stand a better chance of beating the Yankees in a seven-game championship for the free world then they would moving into a new stadium in the foreseeable future."

As the words surely rang in Burke's ears, the owner remembered a night he spent with his father alone on a hill a few years earlier, and a dream stepped boldly to the edges of reality.

Chapter Twenty Eight

If You Come, We Will Build It

Late one night in 1996, Daniel and Frank Burke – father and son – were downtown on the elder's first visit to the Scenic City. When the pair rounded a corner on the banks of the Tennessee River, Burke's father pointed to the top of Hawk Hill – the former site of the Kirkman High School Hawk's football field – and asked, "What are they going to put up there?"

"I don't know," Frank replied.

"I bet a baseball park could fit up there," Daniel said.

Work begins on Hawk Hill.

Though skeptical, certain the site was too small, Frank drove to the base of the hill and watched as his father got out of the car, walked to the top, and paced it off.

"I watched him walking in his London Fog jacket and loafers while I tried to hide under the dashboard, hoping no one would recognize me," Burke said. "He said it would fit. For three years, he kept asking whether I planned to move the park up there. I kept waiting but he kept asking."

For the next four seasons, Burke suffered six-figure losses trying to maintain Engel Stadium, struggling to keep ticket sales even with ever-rising expenses.

In 1998, when it became abundantly clear the city and county wouldn't fund a new stadium, Burke's father came to mind. The Lookouts' owner then had to ask himself the question he'd been posed again and again since his dad took a walk in his London Fog jacket and loafers.

'When will I move the park to Hawk Hill?'

The time to answer that question had come.

After the city rejected Burke's request to finance a stadium, he took his modified request to Mayor Kinsey.

At the end of the pair's discussion, Kinsey agreed to lease the land on Hawk Hill to Burke for 25 years, on the condition Burke build a baseball park on the site.

When the Lookouts' 1998 season rolled to an end just two months after Dortch's editorial claimed the Lookouts had a nearly impossible chance of moving away from Engel Stadium in the next decade, Burke shared his dream with Chattanooga.

If Chattanoogans would come forward and purchase 1,800 season tickets and ten luxury boxes by February 4th, 1999, he would personally finance the construction of a new baseball stadium at the top of Hawk Hill.

For the next 90 days, Burke gave 63 speeches and bartered with the Chattanooga Times Free Press to print order forms for season tickets in the newspaper. He even ran an infomercial on Comcast Cable, plugging the fundraising effort.

"During the ticket drive, I used to do nothing but drive to the post office and look for another order," he said.

On January 28th, just six months after Dortch's editorial stating the Lookouts had a better chance of beating the 26-time World Series champion Yankees in series for the free world, Burke sold the 1,800th ticket. The sale ensured the Lookouts would have a new home by opening day at the start of the new millennium. In total, the franchise sold 14 luxury boxes and 2,063 season tickets.

To celebrate, Burke organized a parade running from the Creative Discovery Museum to the top of Hawk Hill, featuring only Larry and Lumpy, the camels. He dubbed it, "The World's Shortest Parade."

In March, as the Lookouts prepped for their final season in their home at the corner of East Third and O'Neal, construction began on Hawk Hill.

Before crews could start working, four to five feet of dirt was shaved off the top of the hill. Initial plans for the park called for a 5,997-seat stadium, featuring a 400-foot centerfield and a 16-foot high outfield wall, 31 cash registers (nearly triple that at Engel Stadium), twice the restrooms, and an escalator. The project drew a price tag of $10 million.

"Building a stadium is very exhausting," Burke said.

Across town, the Lookouts spent the season in third place as approximately 200,000 fans came out to pay final respects to the home of the team for the past four generations.

"I look at this as a very sad time," season ticket holder Jeff Ballentine told Chattanooga Times Free Press reporter David Jenkins. "Literally, you are losing a piece of history, something not many people have. But change is the only constant in the world; it's up to the fans of Chattanooga to make memories at the new stadium."

Mayor Kinsey guaranteed that Engel Stadium, though

The skeleton of BellSouth Park.

vacant, would be preserved.

"Engel is a place where some of the great names in baseball have played," he said. "We'd never be able to get it back."

Nostalgia didn't draw near the crowd some expected, as the Lookouts saw the smallest crowd at Engel Stadium in a decade. Problems also continued to plague the stadium in its final days as heavy rains flooded the field twice in nine days.

In late August, up on Hawk Hill, Burke faced the skeptics that his park would be done by March with a smile.

"It will be done," he said. "How much do you want to bet? I'm betting $9 to $10 million that it will be."

When the aluminum decking and the steel girders went up in the fall, Burke opened the park to visitors, inviting anyone with interest to come to the new park and watch the construction.

"The night before the opening exhibition game, my dad just sat in the stands watching all the people come to watch us finish the park," he  said. "He told me then that he knew we had something really special here."

On September 9th, one day before the Lookouts played their final game at Engel Stadium – a first-round playoff loss – Burke dedicated the name of the new home of the historic ball club.

The club would play at BellSouth Park.

The Cincinnati Reds made a promise. The big league club, featuring baseball great Ken Griffey, Jr., would come to town and play an exhibition game on March 30th against Cal Ripken, Jr.'s Baltimore Orioles at BellSouth Park.

The game almost mirrored a move made by Joe Engel 70 years before when he brought the Washington Senators to the newly constructed Engel Stadium to play the Lookouts. When the tickets went on sale on a snowy day in December for the big league match-up, 300 people stood in line to reserve their seat. The game sold out completely in just three hours to 6,000 fans.

On the weekend before the exhibition game, Burke opened the stadium to a public tour, showing about 6,000 people around the new park. On the night before the game, Burke scurried around the park from bathroom to bathroom making sure every toilet flushed. Crews with paint brushes were on the field painting the foul pole. Finally, at 2 a.m., everyone left the park just hours before the first pitch.

The day of the game, the seats were packed. The weather served up a beautiful day – sunny and 80 degrees. The famous San Diego Chicken entertained and Kathie Lee Gifford sang the National Anthem. In the luxury box sat Frank's parents with their good friends, former-President George H. and First Lady Barbara Bush, who regularly attended Sea Dogs

games while spending time at their home in Kennebunkport, Maine.

President Bush threw out the opening pitch.

"People accused me of making the Lookouts a political cause because George W. Bush was campaigning for president," Burke said. "I really didn't intend to. I just thought it would be special to invite my dad's friend to this game and surprise him."

Before the game started, some players warmed up and others signed autographs, but Cal Ripken, Jr. followed Burke around BellSouth Park for a behind-the-scenes tour of the Scenic City's new facility.

"He was interested in building a park of his own in Aberdeen, Maryland, so he asked me all kinds of questions about how we built the park," Burke said. "At one point, when I was under the stands showing him how we route the beer through the pipes, I thought, 'Wow! Here I am talking shop with one of the greatest ballplayers of all time!' I actually had to cut him short because I had other things that needed to get done that day. We could have talked all day."

By the end of the game, Burke only heard two criticisms of the Lookouts' new home.

The first came from Ripken.

"He told me there was too much white space on the outfield walls – that the ads interfered with the batter's field of vision," Burke said. "I told him that he'd find out at his park that if you'll sell it, you'll paint it."

The only other complaint seemed to be the most obvious to avoid. At the baseball park sponsored by one of the region's largest telecommunications company, there wasn't even one payphone.

"I thought most people had cell phones so payphones would be obsolete," Burke said.

Quick to rectify the problem, Burke installed three courtesy phones at BellSouth Park, offering free local phone calls to all the guests of the Lookouts.

Offering a bird's eye view of downtown, the park is the perfect place to not just watch a game but look at the mountains above the left field wall, or peek at the Tennessee River and the Aquarium just past the right field line.

Claiming two of the greatest places to watch a game, the Scenic City found baseball again as they had in the glory days of Joe Engel's reign as the king of baseball.

By the end of the 2000 season – the first year on Hawk Hill – the Lookouts attracted 300,000 fans, setting an all-time attendance record for the franchise.

Chapter Twenty Nine

The Old Becomes New

"When you hear that first crack of the bat at batting practice, you know that winter's over."

Spoken like a true fan of the game, Frank Burke is still as much a fan of the national pastime as he is an owner. As a boy, he loved the game because of his dad.

"My dad took me to Detroit Tigers' games when I was 7 years old," he said. "That year, the Tigers won the World Series and my dad taught me to read a box score. I loved it because it was time to spend with my dad at the ball games. Now, I have the greatest job in the world because other dads can spend time with their sons here. I like to think we're not only developing the major league players of tomorrow but also the major league fans of tomorrow."

His focus on the fans is the big reason for the Lookouts' continued success.

"It's all about entertainment," he said. "Every year, we're two or three players in one direction or the other from being a good team or a bad team. Since we have no control over that, we have to make sure people are having a good time."

In 2001, the Reds brought back 1999 head coach Phillip Wellman to lead the Lookouts in their second year at their new home.

Wellman was almost enough entertainment by himself. He was notorious among fans for his colorful disputes with umpires.

"Everybody gets ejected form time to time," Burke said. "Phillip had a gift for it. It didn't matter if we were 78 games behind or three games in front, Phillip was going to wear his heart on his sleeve. He had a passion for his work."

While still coaching at Engel Stadium in 1999, Wellman got sent to the showers when he turned his hat around to block the umpire's face in the midst of the umpire's lecture.

In his first year at BellSouth Park, when a line judge ruled a ball fair that Wellman deemed to be foul, Wellman uprooted third base and moved it a solid foot foul of the third base line. Before he was ejected, he pointed to the bag and looked at the ump, inferring 'Now, it's fair.'

The following season, as the Lookouts claimed the largest opening day crowd in the league for the first time since 1977, Wellman felt the need to re-enact a play. When an opponent was ruled safe after sliding into third base, guarded by Pete Rose Jr., Wellman headed to the bag, pulled Rose's glove off his hand, thumped it down in front of third base, and took a long, headfirst slide right into it. The ump rewarded his improvisation with a trip to the clubhouse.

In his final year with the Lookouts, Wellman was tossed twice more. When second baseman Andrew Beattie was said to be off second base while trying to nail a double play, Wellman took second base off the field and back to the dugout. After the grounds crew installed a new base and the umps booted Wellman, he charged onto the field and took the second bag with him on his long walk to the locker room. Finally, following yet another ejection, Wellman fled to the dugout and threw nine batting helmets onto the field, then slung a baseball toward the left field wall.

Despite his memorable tirades, Wellman wanted fans to remember him for something more before he left in 2004, accepting a job managing a Rookie League club with the Atlanta Braves organization.

"It would be much nicer being remembered for managing a good game instead of making a fool of myself," Wellman said. "Some of those times I had no idea what I was doing."

When he left Chattanooga, Baseball America named Wellman the League's best managerial prospect.

In 2001, the Lookouts played host to their most recent major league prodigy.

After a season in the Rookie Leagues and two more in Single A clubs, Adam Dunn came to Chattanooga for 39 games. He scored 30 times from 48 hits, racking up 12 homers and 31 RBIs, helping Wellman lead the Lookouts to 72 wins and a spot in the playoffs. By mid-May, Dunn led the Southern League in homeruns, runs scored, and on-base and slugging percentages, and was second in RBIs and extra-base hits. Through the first half of the season, he carried a career-high batting average of .343!

Dunn

Triple A Louisville scooped him up and Dunn spent 55 games with the Bats before heading to the majors on July 20th. That December, "ESPN, The Magazine" honored Dunn as just one of two baseball players forecasted to be a future star in their sport. He was the MVP of the Triple A All-Star game and the National League's Co-Rookie of the Month in August. Alongside baseball great Ken Griffey, Jr., in Cincinnati, Dunn and Griffey have united to be the club's best homerun duo in the 133-year history of the organization.

From the front office in 2001, the Lookouts moved into cyberspace, unveiling www.Lookouts.com. On the field, the team played in the post-season for a shot at yet another pennant but were unable to make the dream come true.

The next season, the team slipped to fifth place but fans didn't care and neither did the rest of the nation, finally starting to notice Chattanooga as the re-emerging diamond in the rough.

Baseball America dubbed Chattanooga as the nation's top Double-A franchise.

At the start of the season, the Reds returned to Chattanooga playing the Minnesota Twins in an exhibition game. The game seemed to be a metaphor for Scenic City baseball as the former Washington Senators played the new parent affiliate of the 21st century Lookouts.

In 2003, during Wellman's final year leading the club, attendance dropped. Season ticket sales slipped from 2,000 to 1,400 and three luxury boxes came available. But Burke didn't' flinch.

"Each year becomes more of a challenge because you've got to boost the walk-up crowds to make up for the season tickets," Burke said. "You're going to lose some season tickets year after year because people move, companies merge, or whatever."

Still, Chattanooga is the example for all other club's, according to Southern League President Don Mincher.

"There is always a drop-off in the fourth or fifth years of a new facility but Chattanooga's has been slight and that's a tribute to Frank Burke," Mincher said. "He always has something rolling around in the at mind and he's not a guy who likes to stand around on status quo.

"People looking to own a team have asked me how I would run one and I've told them, 'Go to Chattanooga and see how they do it.'"

The Lookouts finished the year in third place, attracting an average of more than 4,000 fans to 148 games through the season.

With Wellman gone to Danville, Kentucky to lead future Atlanta Braves hopefuls, the Lookouts called on their former catcher – 1999 star, Jayhawk Owens – to lead the club.

During the Lookouts' final season at Engel Stadium, Owens played 47 games as a Lookout. Now, five years later, he returned to the Scenic City and the new ballpark with the perspective of a coach.

"Chattanooga always has a lot of people coming to games and I can see why with this park," Owens said. "Two years ago, I managed in Stockton, California, and we had poor fan support. We were first the entire year and would draw 300 to 400 people per game."

Owens didn't have that same problem in Chattanooga.

The Lookouts finished the season in first place, playing in front of crowds averaging 3,656 fans per game. The club lost to the Tennessee Smokies in the first round of the playoffs.

Owens

The 2005 season marked the 99th season of organized baseball in Chattanooga – from the Roanes in 1880 and the unstable first years of the Southern League, through the legendary era of Joe Engel baseball and the rise and fall of the Southern Association, through the turbulent financial stresses of the club's fall and return through the 1960s, '70s, and '80s.

Burke paid off the debt on the stadium last year – five years ahead of his original ten-year deadline.

"I estimate it will take several years to pay back the equity the investors put into the stadium," Burke said. "Thankfully, we've always taken the approach that the fan was number one, even if that meant spending money on park improvements and fan amenities. That approach will never change as long as I am here."

Burke still treats the park as through it were the first time anyone saw it.

"I pressure wash the stands at the park every night because tonight could be the first night that someone comes to a game," he said.

Though the club slipped to fifth place in 2005, a handful of players stood out.

Kevin Howard led the club with 142 hits through 129 games, scoring 63 times, tallying a team-leading 70 RBIs, and carrying a .296 average.

Norris Hopper led the Lookouts in runs scored – 70 – and triples – 4 through 116 games, posting a .310 average.

Jeff Bannon led the club with fourteen homeruns, scoring 51 times off 97 hits through 93 games. Bannon carried a .266 average when he was called up to Triple A Louisville near the end of the year.

Steve Smitherman led the club with 30 doubles, scoring 45 times off 87 hits through 86 games and carrying a .278 average. He swatted 11 homeruns and 62 RBIs, making him a valuable member of the Lookouts' offense.

On the mound, only two pitchers won more than half of the games they started – Bobby Basham and Adrian Cruz – and just two posted an ERA of less than 3.00 – Basham (2.98) and Ben Weber (2.31).

But just as Burke said, the fans came to BellSouth Park for more than wins and losses.

"That's the sustaining power of baseball," he said. "You can go anywhere in the world and it looks the same. You can enjoy yourself and spend time with someone."

The same $4 that could purchase a general admission ticket in 1995 can buy one today – just another symbol of Burke's commitment to the fans.

"I'm not surprised with anything Frank does because he has an incredible mind," Mincher said. "In Minor League Baseball, the big figures will take care of themselves. It's the little numbers you have to watch out for because those are the things that drive fans away. Fans could care less if a stadium costs $10 million but if you go up on tickets, parking, or concessions, they're going to get upset. I think Frank has always understood this."

Burke seems to be more enthralled with the opportunity to bring the legacy of Lookouts baseball back to Chattanooga.

"We have either introduced or re-introduced the magic of Minor League Baseball to a much larger audience than we ever had at Engel Stadium," Burke said. "We are now seeing people who had their first date at BellSouth Park come back to get engaged in the stadium.

"We have found a whole new generation of fans and they seem to enjoy and appreciate our efforts to make BellSouth Park a wonderful place to be on a summer evening. We are very fortunate that we've been able to make so many friends and they have supported us beyond our wildest dreams."

Burke's unique management style and love for the club makes the Lookouts stand out – rise to the top of more than 200 other minor league teams across 20 leagues in 45 states that attract an annual draw of approximately 40 million fans to minor league parks each year.

The Lookouts are still the diamond in the rough, the gem of the minor leagues and, as Ken Burns stated in his documentary, the club "remains as deeply ingrained in the culture of Chattanooga as barbecue ribs and bread pudding."

"The team is now profitable and its future in Chattanooga is secure," Burke said.

Without a doubt, as long as baseball is the national pastime, the Lookouts will have a home in the heart of Chattanooga.

<u>Legendary</u> <u>Lookouts</u>

While not every former Lookout is bound for Cooperstown, there are still a number of players who once donned a Lookouts jersey, either on their way up to the majors or on their way back down from big league greatness. These are but a few.

<u>Jimmy Bloodworth</u> – Second Base – Born July 26, 1917 – Bloodworth spent 11 seasons in the majors from 1937 to 1951. Through his career, he played with the Senators, Detroit Tigers, Pittsburgh Pirates, Cincinnati Reds, and the Philadelphia Phillies. While with the Lookouts in 1936, Bloodworth set the single game homerun record at three, later tied by Joe Charboneau and Sal Rende. During his major league career, he played 1,002 games, scoring 347 times in 3,519 at bats and hitting 62 career homers, claiming a .248 average. His best year was 1939, carrying a .289 average in 83 games through 318 at bats.

<u>Lloyd Brown</u> - Pitcher – Born December 25, 1904 – Brown spent 12 seasons in the majors from 1925 to 1940. Through his career, he played with the Senators, Brooklyn Robins, Boston Red Sox, St. Louis Browns, Cleveland Indians, and Philadelphia Phillies. Brown played 412 games, posting a 4.27 career ERA, claiming 92 wins, 111 losses and 21 saves. His best year was 1931, posting a 3.20 ERA, gathering 15 wins and 14 losses through 42 games and 0 saves.

<u>"Super" Joe Charboneau</u> – This slugger came to Chattanooga in 1979 carrying a powerful bat. From 1976 to 1978, Charboneau played in Single A clubs for the Philadelphia Phillies and the Minnesota Twins. In Visalia, California, he saw a strong year batting .350 through 130 games and 497 at bats. He scored

119 times off 174 hits, 35 doubles, 5 triples, 18 homers, and 116 RBIs. When he arrived as a Lookout with the Indians organization, he stayed for 19 games. He hit 131 times through 372 at bats and amassed 70 runs - gathering 24 doubles, two triples, 21 homers, and 78 RBIs, boosting his average to .352. Charboneau share the single game homerun record with Sal Rende and Jim Bloodworth, all having hit three in one game. In 1980, he spent a short span of time in Triple A Charleston, West Virginia before heading to the pros where he stayed with Cleveland for three seasons where he hit .266 through 201 games. Today, he's still in baseball coaching in the Frontier League.

Ellis Clary – Clary played four years for the Washington Senators and St. Louis Browns at second and third base, where he swatted a career .263. From 1942 to 1945, he played nearly 200 games carrying an on-base percentage of .376. By the 1950s, Clary was playing infield for the Chattanooga Lookouts and, in 1952, he helped the team win the Southern League Championship. That season he led the team at the bat with a .311 average, earning the title of

Clary

Southern League Most Valuable Player. According to former teammate Roy Hawes, mourners played "Take Me Out to the Ballgame" at Clary's funeral in the late 1990s.

Gil Coan – In 1945, Gil Coan had a record year. While playing for the Chattanooga Lookouts, Coan set the team record for total bases at 345 and tied the total runs scored in a season, set in 1932 by Johnny Gill, at 126. He also set the Southern League record for triples, smacking 28. The next season, Coan was called up to play for the Washington Senators, where he stayed for a single season before coming back to Chattanooga to regroup. By 1948, he had a record season at Washington, scoring 56 times off 119 hits and earning 60 RBIs. In 1951, he repeated another strong season, scoring 85 times off 163 hits and earning 62 RBIs.

Dick Coffman – Pitcher – December 18, 1906 – Coffman spent 15 seasons in the majors from 1927 to 1945. Through his career, he played with the Senators, St. Louis Browns, New York Giants, Boston Bees, and Philadelphia Phillies. Coffman played a total 493 games, posting a career 4.72 ERA, gathering 75 wins, 102 losses, and 39 saves. His best year 1937, posting a 3.04 ERA, claiming 8 wins and 3 losses in 42 games and 3 saves.

Alvin Crowder – Pitcher – Born January 11, 1899 – Crowder spent 11 seasons in the majors from 1926 to 1936. Through his career, he played with the Senators, St. Louis Browns, and the Detroit Tigers. Crowder played 402 games, posting a 4.12 career ERA, gathering 167 wins, 115 losses, and 22 saves. His best year was 1932, posting a 3.33 ERA, claiming 26 wins and 13 losses through 50 games and 1 save.

Charlie Dressen – Third Base – Born September 20, 1898 – Dressen spent eight seasons in the majors from 1925 to 1933. Through his career, he played with the Reds and the New York Giants. Dressen played 646 games, scoring 313 times in 2,215 at bats, nabbing 11 homers and a .272 average. His best year was 1927, carrying a .292 average in 144 games through 548 at bats.

Ed "Patsy" Gharrity – Catcher/First Base – Born March 13, 1892 – Gharrity spent ten seasons in the majors from 1916 to 1930. He spent his entire career with the Senators. Gharrity played 676 games, scoring 237 times in 1,961 at bats, nabbing 20 homers and a .262 career average. His best year was 1921, carrying a .310 average in 121 games through 387 at bats.

Goose Goslin – Outfielder – Born October 16, 1900 – Goslin spent 18 years in the majors from 1921 to 1938. Through his career, he played with the Senators, St. Louis Browns, and the Detroit Tigers. Goslin played a career 2,287 games, scoring 1,483 times in 8,656 at bats, and 248 career homers, carrying a .316 career batting average. His best year was 1928 with the Senators, carrying a .379 batting average through 135 games and 456 at bats.

Kelly Gruber – Third Base – Born February 26, 1962 – Gruber spent two years in Single A clubs before coming to Chattanooga in 1982. Through 128 games, he scored 53 times off 107 hits from 441 at bats, posting a .243 average. In 1984, he burst into the majors with the Toronto Blue Jays, where he spent the majority of his ten-year career. In 1989, 1991, and 1992, Gruber fought with the Blue Jays in the American League Championship game before finally heading to the World Series in 1992, leading to a victory over the Braves and a Series win for the first time in franchise history. When the club repeated its Series victory in 1993, Gruber finished out his final season in the majors with the California Angels, posting a career .259 average through 939 games.

Lee Gutterman – This native son of Chattanooga – born in the Scenic City in 1958 – spent 13 otherwise forgettable seasons pitching in the majors. In 1984, he played for the Lookouts posting a 3.38 ERA and claiming 11 wins from 18 games as the starting pitcher. Through the remainder of his career, his ERA fluctuated between 4.00 and 7.00. However the hometown boy has a unique claim to fame – boasting a lifetime batting average of .500! You see, in 13 seasons, he batted only twice – once for a double and the other, fielding out. He never swung the bat in a game again, leaving his career batting average at an impressive, yet deceptive, .500!

Erik Hanson – The Lookouts' right-hander started his professional career in Chattanooga in 1986, starting his three-year stint in the minors before heading to more than a decade of play in the big leagues. His first season as a Lookout, Hanson played three games posting a 3.86 ERA. The next season, in 1987, he won eight of 18 starts, posting a 2.60 ERA through 21 games. One of the losses was a nose-to-nose duel with the Jacksonville Suns against future Seattle teammate and star, Randy Johnson, that Bill Lee remembers. "In the seventh inning, both were still pitching 97 miles per hour," Lee said. "Normally, we'd go through two or three dozen baseballs a night. That night, we went through nine dozen baseballs because batters only got a piece of them." In midseason, he was called up to Calgary, where he stayed through mid-1988. Through his 11-year career he won 89 and lost 84, posting a career 4.15. In 1995, he appeared in the Red Sox playoff berth, losing the only game he started. He played with the Seattle Mariners, Cincinnati Reds, Toronto Blue Jays, and the Boston Red Sox.

Jackie Hayes – Second Base – Born July 19, 1906 – Hayes spent 14 seasons in the majors from 1927 to 1940. Through his career, he played with the Senators and the Chicago White Sox. Hayes played in 1,091 games, scoring 494 times in 4,040 at bats, nabbing 20 career homers and posting a career .265 average. His best year was 1938, carrying a .328 average through 62 games and 238 at bats.

Jimmy Hitchcock - In 1938 and 1940, Joe Engel helped an All-American Football player chase his Major League Baseball dreams. In the early 1930s, Hitchcock made a name for himself at Auburn Polytechnic Institute (now Auburn University) as he led the Tigers to the Southern Conference championship over the Tulane Green Waves. Also playing baseball at Auburn, and recognizing there was no money during the Great Depression in pursuing a pro-football career, Hitchcock signed with the New York Yankees organization. He spent four seasons with the Yankees and the Pacific Coast League Oakland team before catching the attention of Joe Engel.

In 1938, Jimmy Hitchcock's younger brother, Billy, was making an impression playing baseball at his brother's alma mater. Billy went on to have a long baseball career as a player, coach, manager, and executive. Engel also saw the opportunity to sell a few tickets by hosting a well-known Southern Conference football star on his field.

Hitchcock didn't disappoint.

He played solid shortstop and batted .294 through 114 games.

When the National League Boston Braves came calling, Engel sold the player to the big leagues for Hitchcock's first appearance.

Casey Stengel and Joe Engel.

He struggled from August to September under manager Casey Stengel, who played the career shortstop at second and third base and watched the football star hit only 13 times off his 76 trips to the plate.

In 1940, Stengel sold Hitchcock back to Chattanooga, where he played in the shadow of power-hitters like Bill "Swish" Nicholson and "Babe" Barna.

The next season, Hitchcock wobbled at the Triple A level but saw he'd likely never see the major leagues. He called it quits.

Hitchcock was Auburn's first All-American football player, making his name as tailback. In 1954, he was inducted into the National Football Hall of Fame. He died of a heart attack at just 48 years old in June 1959 before he was inducted into the Helms Football Hall of Fame in 1966.

Sid Hudson – Pitcher – Born January 3, 1915 – Hudson spent 12 seasons in the majors from 1940 to 1954. Through his career, he played with the Senators and the Boston Red Sox. Hudson played 380 games, posting a 4.28 career ERA, gathering 104 wins, 152 losses, and 13 saves. His best year was 1941, posting a 3.46 ERA, nabbing 13 wins and 14 losses through 33 games and 0 saves.

Joe Judge – First Base – Born May 25, 1894 – Judge spent 19 years in the majors from 1915 to 1934. Through his career, he played with the Senators, Brooklyn Dodgers, and Boston Red Sox. Judge played 2,058 games, scoring 1,128 times off 7,493 at bats, 69 homers and posting a career .297 average. His best year was 1920, carrying a .333 average in 126 games seeing 493 at bats.

Jim Kaat – When pitcher Jim Kaat started in Class D baseball for the Washington Senators organization, he was 18 years old. By the time he left baseball in 1983, he was 44 and the owner of 14 American League Gold Glove Awards, two National League Gold Glove Awards and a Word Series Championship ring. He'd played in four playoffs, twice with the Minnesota Twins, once with the Phillies, and the last time with the St. Louis Cardinals when the club won it all in 1982. He also played in three All-Star Games. After two years in Class D and Pioneer League ball, a 20-year-old Kaat came to Chattanooga in 1959 where he won 8 games and lost 8, posting a 16.15 ERA over 24 games. He allowed 126 hits, 71 runs, and posted 61 errors. Despite his rough season with the

Lookouts, he set a single game record of 19 strikeouts and Washington called him up at the end of the season. Kaat lost both games he started and posted a 12.60 ERA. As is evidenced by his career, Kaat got better with age.

Joe Kuhel – First Base – Born June 25, 1906 – Kuhel spent 18 years in the majors from 1930 to 1947. Through his career, he played with the Senators and the Chicago White Sox. Kuhel played 2,104 games scoring 1,236 times in 7,984 at bats, scoring 131 homers and posting a career .277. His best year was 1933, carrying a .322 average in 153 games through 602 at bats.

Stephen Larkin – The Chattanooga Lookouts lent a player to history in the fall of 1998. The brother of legendary Cincinnati Reds shortstop, Barry Larkin, Stephen is a career minor league player with a pacemaker. While playing in Chattanooga in 1998 – his only season with the Lookouts – he played 80 games, scored 33 times off 61 hits and earned 31 RBIs. In August, his pacemaker had a hiccup and the first baseman had surgery to implant a new  one. By the end of September, he was ready to play when the Cincinnati Reds decided to let four brothers have their day. On September 27, 1998, Stephen joined Barry and brothers Bret and Aaron Boone (second and third base, respectively) to play in the only game in the history of the major league to feature an all-brother infield. The Reds beat the Pittsburgh Pirates 4-1. Despite performing better in the game than Barry, hitting one for three compared to his brother's zero for three display, Stephen returned to the minors, never to see major league play again. He took a long absence for the game but re-emerged in 2004 playing for the non-affiliated Northwest League Alexandria Aces and the Atlantic

League Newark Bears. In 2005, he joined the Bridgeport, Connecticut Bluefish in the Atlantic League as an outfielder.

Buddy Lewis – Third Base/Outfielder – Born August 10, 1916 – Lewis spent 11 seasons in the majors from 1935 to 1949. He played with the Senators through his entire career, playing 1,349 games scoring 830 times in 5,261 at bats, posting 71 career homers and a career .297. Lewis' best year 1945 hitting .333 in 69 games through 258 games.

Mickey Livingston – Catcher – Born November 15, 1914 – Livingston spent ten seasons in the majors from 1938 to 1951. Through his career, he played with the Senators, Philadelphia Phillies, Chicago Cubs, Philadelphia Blue Jays, New York Giants, Boston Braves, and the Brooklyn Dodgers. Livingston played 561 games, scoring 128 times in 1,490 at bats, nabbing 19 homers and a career .238 average. His best year was 1946, carrying a .256 average through 66 games and 176 at bats.

Firpo Marberry – Pitcher – Born November 30, 1898 – Marberry spent 14 seasons in the majors from 1923 to 1936. Through his career, he played with the Senators, Detroit, and the New York Giants. Marberry played 551 games, pitching a career 3.63 ERA, winning 148 and losing 88 and getting 101 career saves. His best year was 1926, posting a 3.00 ERA, claiming 12 wins and 7 losses through 64 games and 22 saves.

Edgar Martinez – From 1987 to 2004, third baseman Edgar Martinez swung a very heavy bat, winning the American League Silver Slugger Award six times and playing in six All-Star Games. He spent his entire career with the Seattle Mariners organization, from the date he was drafted to the date he retired. In 1985 and 1986, he spent two seasons in Chattanooga, proving his case to play in the majors. In 1985, at age 22, he scored 43 times off 92 hits, nailing three homeruns and 47 RBIs. After he was unable to get Seattle's attention after 20 games in Triple-A Calgary, he returned to Engel Stadium in 1986, where he scored 79 times off 119 hits, smacking six homeruns and 74 RBIs. Seattle took notice, grabbed Martinez and never let go. He saw playoff berths with the club in 1995, 1997, 2000, and 2001, played in 2,736 games and retired with a lifetime batting average of .312.

"Edgar Martinez was my favorite player but when he was in Chattanooga, he was all field and no hit," said former general manager Bill Lee. "I told that to my friend, Pat, who owned the Mariners, and he said, 'No way.' I had to get Edgar to tell him it was true.

"He was always the first guy to go to player appearances. If you ever needed him to do anything, he was always right there."

Earl McNeely – Outfielder – Born May 12, 1898 – McNeely spent eight seasons in the majors from 1924 to 1931. Through his career, he played with the Senators and the St. Louis Browns. McNeely played 683 games scoring 369 times of 2,254 at bats, four homers and a .272 career average. His best year 1924, carrying a . 330 average through 43 games and 179 at bats.

Bing Miller – Outfielder – Born August 30, 1894 – Miller spent 15 seasons in the majors from 1921 to 1936. Through his career, he played with the Senators, Philadelphia Athletics, St. Louis Browns, and the Boston Red Sox. Miller played 1,666 games scoring 857 times of 5,627 at bats claiming 107 homers and a career .313. His best year was 1924, carrying a .342 average through 113 games and 398 at bats.

Bill Nicholson – Outfielder – Born December 11, 1914 – Nicholson spent 15 seasons in the majors from 1936 to 1953.

Through his career, he played with the Philadelphia Athletics, Chicago Cubs, and Philadelphia Phillies. Nicholson played 1,523 games, scoring 742 in 4,938 at bats, 206 homers and a career .262 average. His best year 1,939, boasting a .295 average through 58 games and 220 at bats.

Donell Nixon – After three years in Single A clubs in the Midwest and California leagues, Nixon came up to Chattanooga in 1984 as part of the Mariners organization. Brother of Cleveland Indians great, Otis Nixon, the 22-year-old Donell batted .269 when he came to Chattanooga, playing 140 games, batting 536 times, and scoring 99 times off 144 hits. Nixon doubled 25 times, tripled five and slugged four homers along with 57 RBIs. That season, he wowed

Nixon nabs another bag in 1984.

Lookouts fans as he set the team's stolen base record, nabbing 102 bases. He sat out the 1985 season, returning to Chattanooga in 1986 for just four games before getting his call to AAA Calgary. The start of 1986, he boasted a strong .333 avg. in his four games, hitting for six of 18 at-bats, scoring twice. In 1987, he made it to Seattle, where he stayed only one season before returning to Calgary, then being sold to the San Francisco Giants. In San Francisco, he saw his only play-off appearance in 1989, one that bore no ring. After his 1990 season, which he spent with the Baltimore Orioles, he retired from baseball.

Warren "Curly" Ogden – Pitcher – Born January 24, 1901 –
Ogden spent five seasons in the majors from 1922 to 1926.
Through his career, he played with the Senators and the
Philadelphia Athletics. For his career, Ogden played 93 games,
posting a 3.79 ERA, claiming 18 wins, 19 losses and 0 saves. His
best year was 1924, posting a 2.75 ERA, gathering nine wins and
five losses through 16 games and no saves.

Marv "Sparky" Olson – Although "Sparky" Olson played
only two seasons in the major leagues for the Boston Red Sox in
1932 and 1933, he was a staple among the minor leagues. In 1933,
he played for the division winning Triple A Newark Bears. In 1936,
he helped the Buffalo Bisons win the International League title. By
1939, he wandered into Chattanooga to hit .280 and help the club
win the 1939 Southern League Championship under manager, Kiki
Cuyler. The next season, Sparky produced a .319 average and the
next he swatted .278. By 1942, when Cuyler left the Lookouts,
Sparky took over as manager of the team. The next season, when
the Lookouts were sold to Montgomery, Alabama, and became the
"Rebels", Sparky stayed by their side, hitting .286. When Engel
brought the club back to Chattanooga in 1944, Sparky came with it
only as a player, hitting .179.

The International League came calling again for Olson in
1945 and, in 1946, he managed the Class D Pony League
Jamestown, New York Falcons to a shared championship – the
result of a tie with another team. Refusing to accept a clouded
victory, Olson led the club to an outright championship the next
season. The club belonged to the Detroit Tigers and they watched
with approval as Olson led the club to two consecutive second-
place finishes the next two seasons. They moved Sparky to Class C
Butler in the Middle Atlantic League in 1950, which he led to a
league championship.

Weary of play, Olson took a job scouting for the Minnesota Twins, which he died from 1962 to 1986. He lived out the rest of his days in Graysville, South Dakota until his death in February 1998.

Ernie Oravetz – Former Chattanooga Times sportswriter Wirt Gammon said Oravetz was one of the best Lookouts ever to field a rebound off the right field wall. The right fielder helped the 1952 team claim the Southern League pennant, carrying a .306 batting average over 144 games. He got his call to the majors in 1955, when he spent two seasons with the Washington Senators. While in Washington, he played 188 games and batted .262.

Val Picinich – Catcher – September 8, 1896 – Picinich spent 17 seasons from 1916 to 1933. Through his career, he played with the Philadelphia Athletics, Washington Senators, Boston Red Sox, Cincinnati Reds, Brooklyn Robins, Brooklyn Dodgers, and the Pittsburgh Pirates. Picinich played 950 games scoring 265 times in 2,609 at bats, slugging 24 homers, and carrying a .256 average. His best year was 1928, carrying a .302 average in 96 games through . 324 at bats.

Lance Richbourg – Outfielder – Richbourg spent eight seasons from 1921 to 1932. Through his career, he played with the Phillies, Senators, Boston Braves, and the Chicago Cubs. Richbourg played 698 games scoring 378 times in 2,619 at bats, nabbing 13 homers and a .308 career average. His best year was 1928, carrying a .337 average through 148 games and 612 at bats.

Kevin Rhomberg – Spending just the 1981 season with Chattanooga, the right-handed batter set single-season records for runs scored – 104 – and hits – 187. Rhomberg also claimed the team's highest single-season batting average at .366, which also led the Southern League. He went on to play three seasons with the Cleveland Indians, hitting .383 through 41 games across three seasons. Today, he's still in baseball coaching in the Frontier League.

Jose Rijo – Sometimes, the minor league farm systems serve as a stark reminder to veteran major leaguers of the hordes of young athletes hungry to take the place of a rusty ballplayer. After leading the Cincinnati Reds to a World Series win in 1990, of which he was named the Most Valuable Player, Rijo's eight-year ERA of 2.84 slipped to a dismal 4.17. Thinking the pitcher needed readjust his performance, the club sent him back to Single-A Dayton, Ohio in 2001, where he pitched a single game. He then came to Chattanooga donning the Lookouts uniform and sitting in the bullpen at BellSouth Park, where he didn't throw a single pitch but watched several young players play hard to take his spot in the big leagues. After six games at Triple-A Louisville, Rijo found his motivation to perform at the major league level. In 2002, the 36-year-old pitched a 2.12 ERA through 13 games – his lowest ERA since he pitched 1.68 through 21 games in 1983 at the tender age of 18. He also received the Tony Conigliaro Award given to players who thrive through adversity. Sometimes, all it takes is one look back to gain a sharper perspective of where you need to be going.

Pete Rose, Jr. – The son of the Cincinnati Reds legend and liar spent three seasons in Chattanooga chasing major league dreams. Despite playing in minor-league parks since 1989, Rose, Jr. has seen Big League action only a single season – 1997. He started that year with the Lookouts as an infielder at Engel Stadium. Swinging for the fences as a member of his dad's organization, he posted a .308 batting average and the Reds gave him the nod. Gaining a base hit at his first at-bat during his first game in Cincinnati, Rose, Jr. thought he'd finally arrived. But his appearance was short-lived. He hit only once more during his next 13 at-bats through 11 games posting an average of .143. He played first and third base for the Reds for three games before he was knocked down to the minors where he still plays today. In 2001 and 2002, Rose, Jr. returned to Chattanooga, playing in BellSouth Park and posting less remarkable batting averages in the low .200s. Rose, Jr., now 36 years old, played the 2004 season with the Colorado Rockies farm system and may see another trip through Chattanooga before he's done. As he told Harold Dow, of CBS' "48 Hours" in a 2000 interview, "I'm a baseball player; it's in my blood. That's the only thing I've ever wanted to do; that's the only thing I've ever thought about doing. I've always wanted to be just like Dad. I know part of my heart's shaped like a baseball." In 2005, Rose Jr., was indicted on federal charges after admitting he distributed steroids to players at Chattanooga after games during the 2001 season.

Deion Sanders – "Neon" Deion Sanders, nicknamed "Primetime" by major sports media, played centerfield for two games as a Chattanooga Lookout in 1995. After playing six seasons in the major leagues with the New York Yankees and the Atlanta Braves – joining the Braves in the World Series against Toronto in 1992 – the Cincinnati Reds purchased Sanders' contract and brought him to Engel Stadium, while he healed from a broken bone and blurred vision in his right eye from a hit sustained while leading the San Francisco 49ers to victory in Super Bowl XXIX. He hit four of the seven times he swung the bat, claiming two RBIs and a homerun, quickly earning a .571 batting average. Sanders' appearance in Chattanooga was cut short when the San Francisco Giants bought his contract that same season and whisked the superstar away to Candlestick Park. During his tenure in professional sports, Sanders also played cornerback in the National Football League, for the Atlanta Falcons, San Francisco 49ers,

Baltimore Ravens, and the Dallas Cowboys, with whom he also won Super Bowl XXX.

Ray Scarborough – Pitcher – Born July 23, 1917 – Scarborough spent ten seasons in the majors from 1942 to 1953. Through his career, he played with the Senators, the Chicago White Sox, Boston Red Sox, New York Yankees, and Detroit Tigers. Scarborough played 318 games, posting a 4.13 ERA, gathering 80 wins, 85 losses and 12 saves. His best year was 1948, posting a 2.82 ERA, claiming 15 wins and eight losses through 31 games and one save.

Charles "Gabby" Street – Street began his baseball career in 1882 as a catcher, eventually working his way to the big leagues with the Cincinnati Reds in 1904. After the 1905 season with the Boston Braves, Street came to Chattanooga as a member of the Lookouts where he stayed until 1908. The Washington Senators called Street back to the majors in 1908, where he served as the yin to future hall-of-fame pitcher Walter Johnson's yang for four seasons. During his first year as a Senator, he caught 137 games, including a string of 16 in nine days. On August 21, 1908, "Gabby" became the first man to catch a baseball dropped from the top of the Washington Monument. By 1920, he started managing minor league clubs in Nashville, Knoxville, Augusta, and Columbia. In 1929, he started the second half of a defining career, managing the St. Louis Cardinals. By the end of his first season as manager, he led the Cards to a league pennant and a loss to the Philadelphia Phillies in the World Series. The next season, the Cardinals met the Phillies in the World Series again, this time claiming the championship. Street spent his remaining years calling play-by-play on the radio for the Cardinals until his death in 1951.

Danny Tartabull – This 1991 major league all-star came through Chattanooga on his way to the majors in 1983. In his only season at Engel Stadium, Tartabull smacked a .301 batting average, scoring 95 times off 145 hits and racking up 17 homeruns. The next year he was called up to Triple-A Calgary before joining the Mariners in Seattle in the mid-1980s. By 1992, Tartabull – then playing for the Kansas City Royals – was the second highest paid player in the majors and, after 12 seasons, grossed nearly $33 million!

Tartabull

Bennie Tate – Catcher – December 3, 1901 – This Whitwell, Tennessee native played ten seasons in the majors from 1924 to 1934. Through his career, he played with the Senators, Chicago White Sox, Red Sox, and Cubs. Tate played 494 games, scoring 362 of 1,330, nabbing four homers, and a .272 average. His best year was 1927, carrying a .313 average through 61 games and 131 at bats.

Sam West – Outfielder – Born October 5, 1904 – West spent 16 seasons in the majors from 1927 to 1942. Through his career, he played with the Senators, St. Louis Browns, and the Chicago White Sox. West played 1753 games scoring 934 times in 6,148 at bats, nabbing 75 homers and a career .299 average. His best year was 1931, hitting .333 in 132 games and 526 at bats.

Mark Wohlers – World Series championship closer Mark Wohlers came to Chattanooga for two games in 1999 – four years after winning a ring with the Atlanta Braves. Wohlers played only two games during the last season of Minor League Baseball played in Engel Stadium. His appearance was less impressive than the five-year 3.54 ERA he posted while in Atlanta. Playing for the Lookouts, he gave up three runs on three errors. The Reds sent the faltering Wohlers to Single-A Dayton from Chattanooga – a move from which he never recovered. His ERA climbed to 4.54 then to 4.79 during the next three seasons before he threw in the towel in 2002. Despite his turbulent decline, Wohlers saw seven play-off runs with arguably two of the best baseball clubs of all time – the New York Yankees and the Atlanta Braves.

Early Wynn – Pitcher – January 6, 1920 – Wynn spent 23 seasons from 1939 to 1963. Through his career, he played with the Senators, Cleveland Indians, and Chicago White Sox. Wynn played 691 games, 3.54 average, 300 wins, 244 losses, and 15 saves. His best year was 1,956, posting a 2.72 ERA, claiming 20 wins and nine losses, through 38 games and two saves.

Lookouts Managers

1901 – Lew Whistler
1902 – Con Strothers
1903 – 1908 – **NO TEAM**
1909 – 1910 – Johnny Dobbs
1911 – 1912 – Billy Smith
1913 – Kid Elberfeld
1914 - 1915 – Harry McCormick
1916 – 1917 – Kid Elberfeld
(NY Highlanders)
1918 – Mike Finn
1919 – 1922 – Sammy Strang
Nicklin
1923 – 1924 - Leslie Nunamaker
1925 – Sammy Strang Nicklin
1926 – Kid Elberfeld
1927 – Jimmy Johnston
1928 – Joe Mathes
1929 – Jimmy Johnston
1930 – Bill Rodgers
1931 – 1933 – Bert Niehoff
1934 – Zinn Beck/Mule Shirley
1935 – Mule Shirley/ Clyde
Milan
1936 – Clyde Milan (Senators)/
Joe B'n'witz/ Alex McCall/ Joe
Engel/ Calvin Griffith
1937 – Clyde Milan/ Bill
Rodgers
1938 – Walter Millies/ Rogers
Hornsby
(St. Louis Cards/Browns,
Boston Braves, Cubs, New York
Giants, Reds)

1939 – 1941 - Kiki Cuyler
1941 – 1943 – Sparky Olson
1944 – Scrappy Moore
1945 – 1947 – Bert Niehoff
1948 – 1949 - George Myatt
(Phillies)
1949 – 1950 – Fred Walters
1951 – Jack Onslow (White Sox)
1952 – 1957 – Cal Ermer
(Twins)
1958 – 1959 – John "Red"
Marion
1960 – Forrest V. "Spark"
Jacobs
1961 – Frank Lucchesi (Phillies,
Rangers, Cubs)
1962 – **NO TEAM**
1963 – 1965 – Jack Phillips
1966 – 1975 – **NO TEAM**
1976 – Rene Lachemann
(Seattle, Milwaukee, Marlins)
1977 – George Farson
1978 – John Orsino/Jimmy
Bragan
1979 – 1981 – Woody Smith
1982 – "Dirty" Al Gallagher
1983 – Allen LaGrant "Mickey"
Bowers
1983 – Bill Haywood
1984 – 1985 – Bill Plummer
(Seattle)
1986 – R.J. Harrison
1987 – Sal Rende

1988 – Tom Runnells (Expos)
1989 – 1991 – Jim Tracy
(Dodgers)
1992 – Dave Miley/Tom Nieto
(2 games)/Ron Oester
1993 – 1994 - Pat Kelley

1995 – Dave Miley (Reds)
1996 – 1998 - Mark Berry
1999 – Phillip Wellman
2000 – Mike Rojas
2001 – 2003 - Phillip Wellman
2004 – 2005 - Jayhawk Owens

Team Standings Through History

Through the past 99 seasons of organized baseball in Chattanooga, the local club has claimed 1st place 19 times, advancing to the playoffs where they won 7 League pennants. Season standings for the history of the club are listed below. Split seasons are designated as follows "Rank/Rank".

1880 – 1884 – 1st (Playing as the Roanes)
1885 – 7th
1886 – 8th (Dropped Out in July)
1887 – 1888 – **NO TEAM**
1889 – 3rd (League Disbanded in July)
1890 – 1891 – **NO LEAGUE**
1892 – 1st/8th
1893 – 7th/4th
1894 – **NO TEAM**
1895 – **CLUB MOVED TO MOBILE**
1896 – 1900 – **NO TEAM**
1901 – 6th
1902 – 6th
1903 – 1904 – **NO TEAM**
1905 – Shreveport club finishes season in Chattanooga, pushed away from home due to Yellow Fever.
1906 – 1908 – **NO TEAM**
1909 – 1st

1910 – 4th
1911 – 5th
1912 – 7th
1913 – 4th
1914 – 6th
1915 – 6th
1916 – 7th
1917 – 6th
1918 – 5th
1919 – 6th
1920 – 8th
1921 – 8th
1922 – 6th
1923 – 7th
1924 – 6th
1925 – 6th
1926 – 6th
1927 – 7th
1928 – 7th/4th
1929 – 8th
1930 – 4th
1931 – 4th
1932 – 1st
1933 – 4th/7th
1934 – 7th/2nd
1935 – 5th

1936 – 7th

1937 – 7th

1938 – 7th

1939 – 1st

1940 – 4th

1941 – 4th

1942 – 7th

1943 – 6th/5th

1944 – 7th/8th

1945 – 2nd

1946 – 3rd

1947 – 4th

1948 – 8th

1949 – 8th

1950 – 7th

1951 – 8th

1952 – 1st

1953 – 6th

1954 – 5th

1955 – 3rd

1956 – 6th

1957 – 4th

1958 – 4th

1959 – 6th/6th

1960 – 8th

1961 – 1st

1962 – **NO TEAM**

1963 – 5th/7th

1964 – 6th

1965 – 7th

1966 – 1975 – **NO TEAM**

1976 – 1st/2nd

1977 – 2nd/2nd

1978 – 5th/3rd

1979 – 4th/3rd

1980 – 4th/4th

1981 – 3rd/4th

1982 – 3rd/5th

1983 – 5th/3rd

1984 – 3rd/4th

1985 – 3rd/5th

1986 – 4th/5th

1987 – 4th/4th

1988 – 1st/2nd

1989 – 4th/5th

1990 – 4th/4th

1991 – 2nd/3rd

1992 – 1st/1st

1993 – 4th/2nd

1994 – 5th/1st

1995 – 2nd/1st

1996 – 3rd/1st

1997 – 2nd/3rd

1998 – 5th/2nd

1999 – 3rd/3rd

2000 – 2nd/5th

2001 – 1st

2002 – 5th

2003 – 3rd

2004 – 1st

2005 – 5th

Versus

"Legendary Rivals"

Through the past 85 seasons, the Chattanooga Lookouts have faced off against hundreds of teams in thousands of games. Inevitably, they faced some formidable foes on their way to greatness in the majors.

For instance, famed Brooklyn Dodger Jackie Robinson and Duke Snider played against the Lookouts in Engel Stadium years ago.

These are but a few others.

Bret Boone – Boone played against the Lookouts with the Jacksonville Suns in 1991 before playing for Chattanooga's parent affiliate, the Cincinnati Reds. He saw the playoffs three times – 1995 with the Reds, 1999 with the Braves, and with Seattle in 2001. He was the National League Gold Glove Award once, the American League Silver Slugger Award twice, the American League Gold Glove Award three times, and played in three All-Star Games.

Scott Brosius – In 1989 and 1990, Brosius played third base against Chattanooga for the Huntsville Stars before going on tow win three consecutive World Series with the New York Yankees, in 1998, 1999, and 2000. He played in the 1998 All-Star Game and won the American League Gold Glove Award in 1999. In their 2001 World Series loss to the Arizona Diamondbacks, Brosius hit two 9th inning game-tying homeruns trying to keep the Yankees dream of a fourth consecutive World Series Championship alive.

Jose Canseco – Before writing a tell-all book about steroid use in the major leagues – of which he admits to playing a major role, implicating himself and several other players and launching a

245

Congressional hearing on the matter in 2005 – Canseco played outfield against the Lookouts with the Huntsville Stars in 1985 and 1989. During his 17-year career wit the Oakland Athletics, he won the American League Silver Slugger Award four times, played in six All-Star Games, named the American League's Most Valuable Player of the Year in 1988 and the American League Sporting News Comeback Player of the Year in 1994. He won two World Series – once with Oakland in 1989 and a second time with the Yankees in 2000.

Chuck Connors – Actor, Chuck Connors, of "Rifleman" and "Branded" played against the Lookouts in 1947, while playing with the Mobile Bay Bears. On one occasion, he hit a homerun during an August game but, during a game in May, Chattanooga police officers had to respond to Engel Stadium after the first baseman had a run-in with fans.

Wil Cordero – In 1989 and 1990, Cordero played shortstop and leftfield with the Jacksonville Suns. In 1994, he won the National League Silver Slugger Award and played in the All-Star Game. He also saw the playoffs with the Cleveland Indians in 1999 and 2001.

Gary Gaetti – In 1981, Gaetti spent a season playing against the Chattanooga Lookouts as an Orlando Ray before spending the bulk of his career in Minnesota. The third baseman hit a homerun in his first at bat in the majors. He won four American League Gold Glove Awards, played in two All-Star games, earned one American League Silver Slugger Award, and was named the Most Valuable Player of the 1987 American League Championship Series, in which the Twins won the World Series. For his career, he batted .255 and played post-seasons wit the Cardinals in 1996 and the Chicago Cubs in 1998.

Jason Giambi – This former Olympian and future All-Star spent 1994 with the Huntsville Stars, going head-to-head against the Lookouts. After playing on the U.S. Olympic baseball team in 1992, Giambi stayed in the minors until 1995 when he was called up to the majors with the Oakland Athletics. Giambi made his name as a New York Yankee playing in four All-Star Games, winning two American League Silver Slugger Awards, and the Hutch Award for spirit and competitive desire. He's been close to winning a championship ring four times, having seen the playoffs twice with Oakland and twice more as a Yankee. Without a doubt, this dog will have his day.

Marquis Grissom – The center fielder spent the majority of his 16-year career with the Montreal Expos but gained most of his accolades playing for the Atlanta Braves when the team won the World Series in 1995. He won the National League Gold Glove Award four times, played twice in the All-Star Game, and was named the1997 American League Championship Series Most Valuable Player with the Cleveland Indians. He saw post-season play in 1995 and 1996 with Atlanta, and 2003 with San Francisco. Grissom battled the Lookouts in 1989 as a member of the Jacksonville Suns.

Bo Jackson – This dual-sport phenomenon started his baseball career, and faced off against the Lookouts, in the Southern Association in 1986 as a rookie with Memphis. He played 53 games, batting .277, before heading to Kansas City to become a staple in the Royals' outfield. Jackson claimed the Heisman Trophy while a runningback with Auburn University and was the first athlete to be named an all-star in two major sports, also gaining celebrity as a runningback with the Los Angeles Raiders – rushing for 2,782 yards on 515 carries. Through his 8-year career in Major

League Baseball, he batted a career .250, hit 141 homeruns, and earned 415 RBIs through 2,393 at-bats and 694 games. After suffering a hip injury during an NFL playoff game in January, 1991, Jackson was forced out of the limelight. He played for the Chicago White Sox for just two seasons before being traded to the California Angels in 1994 – the last year he'd ever play cut short by a player's strike that ended the season. Today, Jackson owns a motorcycle shop outside Chicago, partnered with NBA star, Charles Barkley in owning an Alabama restaurant, and is the president of the Sports Medicine Council – a non-profit, youth outreach of HealthSouth Corporation.

Danny Jackson – In 1982, Jackson pitched against Chattanooga with the Jacksonville Suns before he went on to a 15-year career in the majors. Spending most seasons with the Kansas City Royals and the St. Louis Cardinals, he won the World Series twice – once wit the Royals in 1985 and again in 1990 with the Cincinnati Reds. He played in two All-Star Games and saw the post-season again in 1992 with the Pirates, 1993 with the Phillies, and 1996 with the Cardinals.

Randy Johnson – Arguably one of the greatest pitchers of all time, Johnson threw against the Lookouts in 1987, taking to the mound for the Jacksonville Suns. Johnson spent most of his 17-year career with the Seattle Mariners and the Arizona Diamondbacks posting a career ERA of 3.07 with 246 wins and 128 losses. He saw post-season play six times with Seattle, Houston, and Arizona, including a World Series win in 2001. Nicknamed "The Big Unit", Johnson played in 10 All-Star Games, won the American League Cy Young Award once, four National League Cy Young Awards, and was named the Most Valuable Player of the Word Series in 2001. He struck out 17 or more batters in seven games and once pitched 32 scoreless innings from May 23rd to June

19th, 1997. In 2001, he was named "Sports Illustrated's Sportsman of the Year," which he shared with Curt Schilling. In 2005, he joined the New York Yankees to continue his pitching career.

Chuck Knoblauch – In the span of a decade, the second baseman won four World Series. Knoblauch, who played for the Orlando Rays in 1990, won the World Series with the Twins in 1991 in his rookie season along with being named the American League's Rookie of the Year. He played in five All-Star games, two American League Silver Slugger Awards, and the American League Gold Glove Award in 1997. He went on to win three World Series with the Yankees from 1998 to 2000 and carry a career batting average of .289.

Mark McGwire – A name now synonymous with Babe Ruth and Roger Maris, McGwire spent 1986 – his last season in the minors – with the Huntsville Stars. That year, the slugger hit two homeruns against the Lookouts while playing in Huntsville. Before playing the Lookouts, he was a member of the 1984 U.S. Olympic baseball team. In 1987, he was named the American League's Rookie of the Year. McGwire played in 12 All-Star Games, won two American League Silver Slugger Awards, and one National League Silver Slugger Award along with the Lou Gehrig Award. In 1989, he won the World Series with the Athletics and, nearly a decade later, shattered Roger Maris' single-season homerun record of 61 with an astonishing 72. In 1998, he was named "Sports Illustrated's Sportsman of the Year," alongside homerun record-chaser Chicago Cub, Sammy Sosa.

Hideo Nomo – In 1995, a Japanese phenom burst into major league baseball wit the Los Angeles Dodgers. Nomo took the mound and led the Dodgers to see the playoffs for two consecutive seasons. He was named the National League's Rookie of the Year and played in the 1995 All-Star Game. However, four years later, his pitching slipped, dragging his career ERA to 4.05 and landing Nomo in Double-A Huntsville in 1999. While he's never returned to his inspiring level of play seen in his rookie season, Nomo continues to pitch for the Tampa Bay Devil Rays.

Cal Ripken, Jr. – While playing for the 1980 Southern League Champion Charlotte Orioles, Cal Ripken, Jr. came to Engel Stadium and smacked two homeruns during separate road trips. Ripken, Jr. spent his entire 21-year career wit the Orioles organization. He won eight American League Silver Slugger Awards, two American League Gold Glove Awards, was named Most Valuable Player of the American League twice, played in 19 All-Star Games (of which he was named Most Valuable Player twice) and was the American League Rookie of the Year in 1982. He won the Lou Gehrig Award in 1992 and was named "Sports Illustrated's Sportsman of the Year in 1995." He saw post-season play in 1983, 1996, and 1997. In 2004, the Orioles retired his jersey - #8. In 2000, Ripken, Jr. came back to Chattanooga to play an opening day exhibition game against the Lookouts' parent-affiliate Cincinnati Reds at the newly constructed BellSouth Park.

John Rocker – The notorious Atlanta Braves pitcher was eventually released from the team for making racist remarks and giving offensive hand gestures to the Turner Field crowds. He played the 2003 season with the Orlando Rays. After seeing post-season play in 1998, 1999, and 2000, he carried a career ERA of 3.42.

Alex Rodriguez – Seattle's slugging shortstop played against the Lookouts in 1994, as a member of the Jacksonville Suns. Rodriguez spent most of his 11-year career in Seattle, posting a .305 career batting average. He won the American League Silver Slugger

Award seven times, played in eight All-Star Games, won the Hank Aaron Award for best overall hitter three times, two American League Gold Glove Awards, and was named the Most Valuable Player of the American League in 2003. Rodriguez continued to play as of 2005 with the New York Yankees.

Bret Saberhagen – Before winning the 1985 World Series with the Kansas City Royals, Saberhagen played against the Lookouts with the Jacksonville Suns in 1983. The pitcher boasted a 16-year career ERA of 3.34. In only his second year in the majors, he was named the World Series Most Valuable Player. He won the American League Cy Young Award twice, played in three All-Star Games, and was named the American League Sporting News Comeback Player of the Year in 1987 and again in 1998. In 1989, he pitched 32 consecutive scoreless innings and, in 1991, won the Tony Conigliaro Award for thriving through adversity.

Terry Steinbach – Steinbach spent two seasons as a Huntsville Star in 1985 and 1986 before heading on to play three major league All-Star games and win the 1989 World Series with the Athletics. In 1988, he was voted the Most Valuable Player of the All-Star Game and, during his first major league at-bat in 1986, he hit a homerun. During the course of his 14-year career, he saw the playoffs four times – all with Oakland – and posted a career batting average of .271.

Andy VanSlyke – The 12-year veteran spent most of his career with the Pittsburgh Pirates playing outfield. He won the National League Silver Slugger Award twice, the National League Gold Glove Award five times, and played in three All-Star Games. In 1993, he played against Chattanooga as a member of the Carolina Mudcats.

Tim Wakefield – In 1993, Wakefield pitched against the Lookouts with the Carolina Mudcats. During his 12-year career, spent mostly with the Boston Red Sox, he claimed 128 wins, 111 losses, enjoyed a World Series victory with Boston in 2004, and was named the American League Sporting News Comeback Player of the Year in 1995. He also played in the postseason in 1992 and the Pittsburgh Pirates and 1995, 1998, 1999, and 2003 with Boston.

Walt Weiss – More than half the seasons Weiss played in the majors, he spent in the playoffs. The shortstop, who made his debut with the Athletics in 1987, spent 1986 and part of 1987 with the Huntsville Stars. Weiss was the American League's Rookie of the Year in 1988 and won the World Series with Oakland in 1989. After playing post-seasons with the Athletics in 1990 and 1992, he saw more post-season action with the Colorado Rockies in 1995. He saw the All-Star Game again in 1998, while playing wit the Atlanta Braves, with whom he saw three more playoffs in 1998, 1999, and 2000. He retired with a career batting average of .285.

Historic Lookouts Driving Tour

Many of the poignant locations prominent in Chattanooga Lookouts history are still standing today or are commemorated in various places throughout the city. See these special places yourself following this driving tour through the legacy of Lookouts baseball!

START
400 Chestnut Avenue – Chattanooga Regional History Museum
The museum features unique photos and memorabilia through Lookouts history, including a video interview with Jackie Mitchell!

NEXT – 201 Power Alley – BellSouth Park
Proceed down Chestnut Street to West 3rd Street and turn left. At the top of the hill, you'll find BellSouth Park; the current home of the Chattanooga Lookouts! If you're in town between April and September, stop in and catch a game!

NEXT – Douglas and Vine Street – The First Ball Park
Turn left onto Chestnut Street from Power Alley and proceed to Riverside Drive. Turn right on Riverside Drive and proceed approximately four miles to Mabel Street, then turn right. Turn right again on Douglas Street and proceed to the corner of Douglas and Vine streets. The site of Maclellan Gym, on the University of Tennessee at Chattanooga campus, was the home of the first ball park to host professional baseball in the Scenic City.

NEXT – 1130 East Third Street – Engel Stadium/Andrews Field
Turn left on Vine Street, then left on Central Avenue. Take a right on East 3rd Street and then a right on O'Neal Street. This intersection is the home of Historic Engel Stadium, and the former site of Andrews Field.

NEXT – 1400 Market Street - The Stanton House/Stanton Field
Turn right onto East 3rd Street to North Holtzclaw Avenue. Turn
right on North Holtzclaw Avenue to East Main Street. Turn right
on East Main Street to Market Street. Turn right on Market Street
and proceed to the 1400 block to the site of the Chattanooga Choo
Choo Holiday Inn and Convention Center. This was the former
site of the Stanton House and, behind it, Stanton Field.

NEXT – 1 Rivermont Road – The 1936 House Giveaway
Turn right on Market Street and proceed to Martin Luther King
Boulevard. Turn left on Martin Luther King and proceed to
Highway 27. Enter Highway 27 northbound and proceed to
Manufacturers Road. Exit at Manufacturers Road and turn left,
proceeding to Cherokee Boulevard. Turn right onto Cherokee and
proceed along this roadway. It will turn into Frazier Avenue, then
Barton Avenue, and finally Hixson Pike. Follow Hixson Pike to
Rivermont Road and turn right. The first house on the left is the
house given away in the 1936 house giveaway at Engel Stadium.

NEXT – 122 North Crest Road – T.R. Preston's House
From Rivermont Road, turn right onto Hixson Pike and proceed to
Highway 153. Turn right on Highway 153 southbound and proceed
to Shallowford Road. Turn right after you exit and follow
Shallowford Road to Wilcox Blvd. Turn left on Shallowford Road
and follow Usher Raymond Parkway to the top of Missionary
Ridge, where you'll turn right on North Crest Road. The house will
be on the right, and is constructed using many of the bricks from
the Stanton House when it was razed in the early 1900's.

NEXT – 660 Julian Road – Joe Engel's former home and ranch
From Shallowford Road, head back to Highway 153. Turn right on
Highway 153 southbound and proceed to Interstate 75. Take 75

southbound and proceed to the East Brainerd Road exit, then turn left. Follow East Brainerd Road to Graysville Road and turn right, then right again on Dudley Road. Proceed to Julian Road and then turn left. Look for the large, concrete baseballs at the top of a large stone fence at the end of the driveway about a quarter mile before you reach Council Fire Golf Course. These stone walls mark the property line for Engel's horse farm and house.

END – Back to Chattanooga Regional History Museum
Turn left on East Brainerd Road and proceed to Interstate 75. Take Interstate 75 southbound to Interstate 24 westbound. Proceed to Highway 27 northbound and take the Martin Luther King Boulevard. Exit, then turn right onto Martin Luther King. Take a left onto Chestnut Street and you'll return right where you started at the Chattanooga Regional History Museum.

INDEX

A

B

Chattanooga Warriors – 20-21
Chattanooga White Sox – 34-35, 37, 39
Chief Lookout - 201
Cincinnati Reds – 44, 49, 183, 189, 198, 212, 215, 218, 222, 224,
226, 229, 234-237, 239-241, 244, 246, 248
Clark, George Cunningham "Mudball" - 22
Clark, Jeff – 22
Clarke, Fred - 77
Clarkson, Art – 176
Clary, Ellis – 113, 115, 123, 223
Cleveland Indians – 39-40, 77, 100, 160-161, 170-171, 174, 222,
223, 232, 235, 239, 245-246
Coan, Gil - 223
Coca-Cola – 22, 182, 190
Coffman, Dick - 224
Colavito, Rocky - 135
Connors, Chuck - 245
Cooperstown, National Baseball Hall of Fame – 12, 31, 40, 64, 68,
74, 90, 94, 111-112, 117, 136, 154, 160, 222
Cordero, Wil - 245
Coveleskie, Harry – 27
Creative Discovery Museum - 210
Crittenden, Jim – 162, 169-175
Cronin, Joe – 48, 86
Crosby, Bing – 49
Crowder, Alvin - 224
Cruz, Adrian - 220
Cuyler, Hazen Shirley "Kiki" – 90-94, 98-99, 199, 233, 240

D

Davidson, Bill - 197
Davis, Alvin – 174-175

Davis, Eric - 198

Dean, Dizzy – 39, 41, 105

Del Rosario, Maximo - 188

Delmer, Deacon - 129

Dempsy, Jack - 70

DiMaggio, Joe – 39, 71, 73, 103-105, 108

Dixie Series – 25, 77, 79

Dixie Trophy - 128

Dobbs, Johnny – 25, 240

Donovan, Richard – 35, 37-38, 272

Dortch, Chris – 208, 211

Dressen, Charlie - 225

Dunn, Adam – 217

Durocher, Leo – 110

Dziadura, Gene - 151

E

Eisenhower, Dwight D. - 130

Elberfeld, Norman Arthur "Tabasco Kid" – 25-27, 29, 31-33, 42, 59, 68, 75, 240

Eldridge, David – 148, 158

Eldridge, Mary - 158

Engel, Joseph Bryant - 76

Engel, Joseph William – He was the captain of the Lookouts for 35 years, setting the bar for what Chattanooga baseball has become. Engel is named in more than 75 percent of this book. The stadium still bears his name. This book could easily be titled, "Joe Engel & 100 Seasons of Scenic City Baseball."

Engel Stadium – 46, 49, 51, 55, 57, 59, 62-63, 65, 68, 71, 75, 81, 83, 95, 97-98, 108, 118-119, 124-125, 127, 131-132, 134, 136, 139, 141, 145, 148-149, 156-157, 160-164, 166, 168-171, 178, 180, 182-186, 189, 192-193, 195-200, 203-206, 209-212, 216, 218, 221, 231, 235-236, 238-239, 244-245, 248, 251-252

Erlanger Hospital – 25
Ermer, Calvin Coolidge – 113-117, 119, 123, 159-160, 240
Eshbach, Charles - 203
Exum, Roy – 205-206

F

Feller, Bob – 100
Ferrel, Eddie - 89
Fields, Charley – 148
Finley, Brian - 188
Finley, Charles - 162
Finn, Mike – 32, 240
Fisher, Newt – 22
Friar, Del – 123
Forest Hills Cemetery – 159, 185
Frank, Charley – 22

G

Gaetti, Gary - 245
Gammon, Wirt – 18, 24, 83, 159, 234
Gammon Jr., Wirt – 6
Garbous, Glen – 118
Gehrig, Lou – 55-57, 59, 63-68, 95, 136, 248
Gharrity, Ed "Patsy" – 224
Giambi, Jason - 246
Gifford, Kathie Lee - 213
Gonzalez, Waldo – 137-138
Goslin, Goose – 48, 225
Grady, Henry W. – 15
Graf, Fred – 28-30, 159
Grate, Don – 113, 115-118, 127
Greater Chattanooga Sports Committee - 199
Greenville Braves – 187-188

Griffith, Calvin – 86, 88, 131-132, 135, 138-139, 142-143, 157, 240
Griffith, Clark – 27, 44-48, 51-52, 77-78, 86-87, 91, 131-133, 199
Griffith Stadium – 100-102, 131
Griffey Jr., Ken – 212, 217
Grimes, Burleigh – 28-32, 199
Grissom, Marquis - 246
Gruber, Kelly - 225
Guglielmo, Augie – 53
Gutterman, Lee - 225
Guy, Jonathan (J. Guy Photo) – 2, 5

H

Haley, Bud - 34
Hall, Bill – 6
Hallieboy – 118
Hammond Organs – 164, 189
Hammond, Chris – 187, 189
Hanson, Erik - 226
Hart, Billy – 14
Hawes, Roy – 5, 44, 114, 116, 120, 122, 126, 129, 134, 136, 140, 144, 223
Hawk Hill – 209-211, 214
Hayes, Jackie - 226
Haywood, Bill – 174, 241
Heise, James - 138
Hemsley, Rollie – 89-90
Herman, Alex – 34-36, 38
Herman, Paul – 119, 141, 164
Hightower, Mims – 23
Hitchcock, Billy – 162, 166-167
Hitchcock, Jimmy – 227-228
Hixson, W.C. – 34
Hodges, Gil – 145

I

J

Jones, Johnny – 53
Jordan, Michael – 199
Judge, Joe - 228

K

Kaat, Jim – 228-229
Killebrew, Harmon Clayton – 132-137, 199
Kinsey, John – 205, 210-211
Kinsey, Kim – 6
Kinston Indians – 11
Kirkman High School - 209
Knoblauch, Chuck - 249
Knothole Gang – 51, 142, 172
Kuhel, Joe - 229

L

Lanahan, Dick - 93
Landis, Judge Kenesaw Mountain – 32, 37, 39, 66, 68, 76, 101
Landreth, Harry – 173-176, 180, 195
Langston, Mark – 174-175
Larkin, Barry - 229
Larkin, Stephen - 229
Larry and Lumpy, the camels – 204, 211
Lasko, Bob – 149-150
Layne, Hillis – 3, 5, 58, 95, 98, 101-103, 107, 159, 164
Lazerri, Tony – 66-67
Lee, Bill – 6, 68, 178-183, 186, 190-195, 197, 226, 231
Levan, Jess – 137-138
Lewis, Buddy - 230
Livingston, Mickey - 230
Lockhart, Keith – 187, 189
Loggia, Robert - 180
Looie, the Lookout - 201

Lookout Billiard Hall – 30
Lookout Juniors - 68
Lookout Recreation Hall - 30
Lookout Valley - 14
Lookouts – 1, 2, 5, 12, 18, 24-32, 34, 35, 37, 42, 45-46, 50-53, 55-57, 61, 63, 65-66, 71, 73, 75-79, 81, 86, 88, 90, 92-95, 97, 99, 101, 108-109, 112, 114, 116-120, 123-124, 126, 128-132, 134, 136-154, 156-157, 160, 163-165, 166, 168-174, 176-184, 186-189, 193, 195, 197-200, 202-207, 209-224, 226, 229, 232-237, 239-240, 244-248, 250, 253
Lookouts Booster Club – 142-144, 149, 156, 160
Lookouts Youth Foundation – 143, 147-149
Louise, the Lookouts Fan - 205
Louisville Bats – 217, 220, 224, 235
Lovell Field - 164
Lucchesi, Frank – 146, 241
Lum and Abner Radio Show - 72

M

Maclellan Gym – 14
Mann, Earl – 159
Masingill, Luther – 92, 159
Marberry, Firpo - 230
Marion, John "Red" – 137-138, 241
Maris, Roger – 55, 247-248
Marshall, Rube – 22
Martin Hotel, The - 109
Martin, Jelly Roll – 39
Martinez, Edgar – 230-231
Martini, Tina – 5
Martini, Tony – 5
Martini, Tonya – 5
Martini, Zachary – 5

Mays, Willie – 107-112, 118

McAdams, Ralph - 93

McCallie School - 70

McCormick, Harry – 31, 240

McDaniels, Skeet – 98

McDonald, Arch – 70-75, 78, 100

McElreath, Allen – 92-93

McGaughy, Judge William – 51

McGwire, Mark – 55, 249

McNeely, Earl - 232

Mitchell, Clarence - 130

Mitchell, Virnett Jackie – 57-60, 62-68, 130, 251

Miller, Bing - 231

Miller, Glenn – 13

Mills, Charlie – 82-83

Mincher, Don – 218, 220

Minnesota Twins – 74, 114, 136, 139, 145, 157-158, 218, 222, 229, 234, 240, 250

Mobile Bay Bears - 244

Mobile Pastimes – 14, 16-18, 21, 28, 76, 242

Mobile Tigers – 34

Montague, Carrington - 181

Montemayor, Felipe – 126, 129

Montreal Expos - 145

Moon Pie – 25

Morris, Allen – 159, 161

Morrow, Charles "Buck" - 52

Mullenhauer, Bob – 164-165

Murphy, Dwayne – 165-166, 168

Murtaugh, Danny - 129

Musial, Stan - 104

Myer, Buddy – 48

N

NAACP - 130

Nashville Sounds - 193

Nashville Vols – 14, 16, 19, 22, 87, 90-93, 116, 141-142, 157, 237

Negro League – 32, 34, 38-41, 49, 131

Negro American League – 107

Negro Southern League – 107-108

Nelson, Craig T. - 180

New Orleans Pelicans – 17-18, 21-22, 93, 116, 126

New Orleans Black Pelicans – 39

Newville, Todd - 77

Neyland, General Robert - 17

Nicklin, Sammy Strang – 17, 32-33, 37, 240

Nicholson, Bill – 92, 228, 232

Niehoff, Bert – 60, 76, 240

Nixon, Donell - 232

Nobles, Tom – 53

Nolan, Paul – 186

Nomo, Hideo – 249-250

Notre Dame High School - 143

Nunamaker, Leslie – 32, 240

O

Oakland Athletics – 162, 164-165, 169-170, 248-249

O'Brien, Pat "Midnight" a.k.a. Captain Dynamite – 196

Oester, Ron – 187, 189, 241

Ogden Raptors – 11

Ogden, Warren "Curly" - 232

Oldis, Bob – 115-116

Olgiati, P.R. – 132, 141

Oliver, Joe – 187-189

Olson, Marv "Sparky" – 233, 240

Reid, Sarah - 162
Reid, Woodrow – 162, 164, 166-167, 169-171
Reingold, Arvin – 6, 162
Reyna, Luis - 188
Rhomberg, Kevin – 173, 235
Richbourg, Lance - 234
Richey, Joyce – 6
Rickey, Branch – 42-43, 46
Rickey, Branch III – 186
Rijo, Jose - 235
Ripken Jr., Cal – 212-214, 250
Roacho, the Clown - 201
Robinson, Jackie – 39, 46, 244
Robinson, Wilbert – 30
Rocker, John - 250
Rocky, the Raccoon - 201
Rodgers, Bill "Rawmeat" – 140, 240
Rodriguez, Alex – 250-251
Roesler, Mike - 187
Roosevelt, President Theodore – 46, 101
Rose Jr., Pete – 216, 236
Rosten, Leo – 5
Runnels, Tom - 186
Ruth, Babe – 31, 41, 47, 55-57, 59-60, 62-65, 67-68, 73, 95-96, 200, 247
Ryan, Nolan - 100

S

Sacka, Frank – 125-126
SALLY (South Atlantic) League – 24, 147-149
Salt Lake City Buzz – 11
San Diego Chicken - 213
Saberhagen, Bret - 251

Sanders, Bob – 148

Sanders, Deion – 236-237

Sandlin, Davis – 118-119, 140

Sandlin, Eleanor – 119, 140

Satchel Paige All-Stars - 39

Scarborough, Ray – 236-237

Schott, Marge – 186, 198

Seattle Raniers - 104

Seattle Mariners – 98, 174-175, 182-183, 226, 231, 233, 238, 241, 245-247

Seminick, Andy - 150

Sequatchie Valley Baseball League – 96

Shepherd, Beck – 107, 109

Short, George – 140-141

Short, Rob - 145

Smith, Billy – 25, 240

Smith, Mike – 187-189

Smith, Sam – 148-149

Smith, Woody - 240

Smitherman, Steve - 220

Society of American Baseball Research - 105

Southeastern Conference - 206

Southern League – 17-22, 38-39, 71, 79, 91, 107-108, 139, 149, 162-163, 166, 168, 173, 176, 179, 187, 189-190, 217-219, 223, 233-235, 244

Southern Association – 22-23, 25, 28, 31-32, 73, 75-77, 83, 92, 108, 115, 120, 123, 137, 141-143, 147, 149, 153, 199, 219

Southern Railway – 23-24

Spink, J.G. Taylor – 40

Sporting News, The – 40, 60, 71, 116, 154, 167, 245, 249-250

St. Louis Cardinals – 43-44, 46, 229, 237-238, 246, 250

Stanton, John C. – 15-17, 20-23

Stanton House – 15, 21-24

W

Y

BIBLIOGRAPHY

Web Sites

- Ball Park Reviews.com 1 May 2005.
<http://www.ballparkreviews.com/chatt/engel.htm>
- Baseball Cube. 1 May 2005.<http://www.thebaseballcube.com/>
- Baseball Pilgrimages 1 May 2005.
<http://www.baseballpilgrimages.com/AA/chattanooga.html>
- Brainy Media. 1 May 2005. <http://www.brainyhistory.com>
- www.baseball-almanac.com
- The Chattanoogan. 1 May 2005. <http://www.chattanoogan.com>
- Chattanooga Lookouts. 1 May 2005. <http://www.lookouts.com>
- Cornerstones, Inc. 1 May 2005.<http://www.cornerstonesinc.org>
- Greenfield Historical Society. 1 May 2005.
<http://www.greenfieldhistoricalsociety.org>
- Hill Street Press. 1 May 2005.
<http://www.hillstreetpress.com/CrackersFeature.html>
- National Baseball Hall of Fame and Museum. 1 May 2005
<http://www.baseballhalloffame.org>
- Minor League Ballparks.com 1 May 2005.
<http://www.minorleagueballparks.com/enge_tn.html>

Books

Burns, Ken. Baseball. New York, New York. Alfred A. Knopf, Inc., 1994
Pages 144-149, 169, 173, 179, 197, 201-202, 206, 258, 268, 321, 334

Cataneo, David. Peanuts and Crackerjack: A Treasury of Baseball Legends
and Lore. Nashville, Tennessee. Rutledge Hill Press, 1991 – Pages 10, 26,
102-103, 152, 162, 236, 253, 260-262, 265

Diamondback Communications, ed. Minor Miracles: The Legend and
Lure of Minor League Baseball; South Bend, Indiana. Diamondback
Communications, Inc., 1995 – Pages 169-183

Einstein, Charles. The Baseball Reader: Favorites from the Fireside Books
of Baseball; New York, New York. Bonanza Books, 1989

Reprinted from a 1953 issue of Collier's article entitled "The Fabulous Satchel Paige" by Richard Donovan; Crowell-Collier Publishing Company. – Page 75-76, 83, 89-90, 93, 95-97

Gammon, Wirt. Your Lookouts Since 1885; Chattanooga, Tennessee. Chattanooga Publishing, Co., 1955

Kahn, Roger. Memories of Summer: When Baseball Was an Art, and Writing About It a Game. New York, New York. Hyperion, New York, New York, 1997 – Pages 7-8, 15, 151-154

Koppett, Leonard. The Man in the Dugout: Baseball's Top Managers and How They Got That Way. New York, New York. Crown Publishers, Inc., 1993 – Pages 119, 146, 187

Nash, Bruce and Allan Zullo. The Baseball Hall of Shame 4. New York, New York. Pocket Books, 1990 – Pages 55, 95

Shearer, John. Chattanooga Trivia. Signal Mountain, Tennessee. Mountain Press, Inc., 2000 – Pages 25, 43-47, 57, 82, 112-114

The Sporting News, ed. Baseball's Hall of Fame, Cooperstown: Where the Legends Live Forever. New York, New York. Arlington House, Inc., 1983 – Pages 63, 102, 103, 115-116, 164-165, 185, 187-188, 206-207, 249, 313-314

Wilson, John. Chattanooga's Story; Chattanooga, Tennessee. Roy McDonald, Publisher, 1980 – Pages 323, 325, 357-358, 395, 397, 446

PHOTO INDEX

Page 108 – "Willie Mays as a Chattanooga Choo Choo" – Courtesy of the Chattanooga Regional History Museum

Page 110 – "Mays Hall of Fame Plaque" – Courtesy of the National Baseball Hall of Fame

Page 114 – "Grate Comes Home" – Courtesy of the Chattanooga Lookouts

Page 115 – "Cal Ermer" – Courtesy of Topps, Inc.

Page 118 – "Grate's Record Throw" – Courtesy of the Greenfield Historical Society

Page 121 – "Roy Hawes and his Bride" – Courtesy of Roy Hawes

Page 125 – "Fans in the Stands" – Courtesy of the Chattanooga Lookouts

Page 134 – "Harmon Killebrew" – Courtesy of the Chattanooga Regional History Museum

Page 136 – "Killebrew Hall of Fame Plaque" – Courtesy of the National Baseball Hall of Fame

Page 147 – "1961 Lookouts" – Courtesy of the Chattanooga-Hamilton County Bicentennial Library

Page 152 – "Jenkins Hall of Fame Plaque" – Courtesy of the National Baseball Hall of Fame

Page 154 – "Ferguson Jenkins" – Courtesy of CMGWorldwide.com

Page 157 – "The Longest Winter" – Courtesy of the Chattanooga Lookouts

Page 159 – "Engel's Office" – Courtesy of the Chattanooga-Hamilton County Bicentennial Library

Page 159 – "A.L. Bender" – Courtesy of Chattanooga.gov

Page 160 – "Engel's Headstone" – Courtesy of Dry Ice Publishing

Page 166 – "Denny Walling" – Courtesy of Woodrow W. Benefield

Page 169 – "Lookouts at Bat" – Courtesy of Woodrow W. Benefield

Page 173 – "Players and Umps" – Courtesy of the Chattanooga Lookouts

Page 175 – "Mark Langston" – Courtesy of the Chattanooga-Hamilton County Bicentennial Library

Page 176 – "Alvin Davis" – Couresty of the Chattanooga-Hamilton County Bicentennial Library

Page 179 – "Bill Lee" – Courtesy of the Chattanooga Lookouts

Page 189 – "1988 Pennant Win" – Courtesy of the Chattanooga-Hamilton County Bicentennial Library

Page 192 – "Engel Renovation" – Courtesy of the Chattanooga Lookouts

Page 194 – "Engel Stadium" – Courtesy of the Chattanooga Lookouts

Page 194 – "Engel Field Renovation" – Courtesy of the Chattanooga Lookouts

Page 197 – "Captain Dynamite" – Courtesy of the Chattanooga Lookouts

Page 198 – "Old and New Logos" – Courtesy of the Chattanooga Lookouts

Page 199 – "1992 Lookouts" – Courtesy of the Chattanooga Lookouts

Page 202 – "Cheering the Lookouts" – Roacho, Chief Lookout, and Pop-Up – Courtesy of the Chattanooga-Hamilton County Bicentennial Library; Rocky, the Raccoon and classic Looie – Courtesy of the Chattanooga Lookouts; Looie, the Lookout – Courtesy of J. Guy Photo

Page 203 – "Frank Burke" – Courtesy of J. Guy Photo

Page 205 – "Larry and Lumpy the Camels" – Courtesy of the Chattanooga Lookouts

Page 208 – "Engel Concourse Renovation" – Courtesy of the Chattanooga Lookouts

Page 210 – "Hawk Hill Construction" – Courtesy of the Chattanooga Lookouts

Page 212 – "BellSouth Park Construction" – Courtesy of the Chattanooga Lookouts

Page 212 – "BellSouth Park Field" – Courtesy of the Chattanooga Lookouts

Page 214– "San Diego Chicken v. Barney" – Courtesy of the Chattanooga Lookouts

Page 214 – "Kathie Lee Gifford" – Courtesy of the Chattanooga Lookouts

Page 218 – "Adam Dunn" – Courtesy of the Cincinnati Reds

Page 220 – "Jayhawk Owens" – Courtesy of J. Guy Photo

Page 224 – "Ellis Clary" – From "Your Lookouts Since 1885" by Wirt Gammon

Page 228 – "Engel and Stengel" – Courtesy of the Chattanooga Lookouts

Page 230 – "Stephen Larkin" – Courtesy of the Bridgeport Bluefish

Page 233 – "Donell Nixon" – Courtesy of the Chattanooga Lookouts

Page 239 – "Danny Tartabull" – Courtesy of the Chattanooga Lookouts

CHECK OUT MORE TITLES

BY STEPHEN MARTINI

Fiction Titles

Far From Gilded Halls – The true-to-life historical fiction novel following the life and love story of Johnny Appleseed – an American hero.

ISBN - 1-4116-0814-3

Non-Fiction Titles

Finally, Martini Time – A collection of opinions taken from more than fifty editorials written for The Daily Mississippian: the student-produced newspaper of the University of Mississippi.

Buy online at www.dryicepublishing.com

Or

Pre-order your next copy by e-mailing us at

info@dryicepublishing.com

[When ordering, include name, address, telephone number and payment information. Visit our Web site for individual retail prices. Discounts are available for bulk orders on all Dry Ice Publishing titles.]

VISIT US ONLINE @

WWW.DRYICEPUBLISHING.COM

WHEN YOU VISIT OUR WEB SITE, YOU'LL GET:

- *AUTHOR TOUR INFORMATION*

- *JOURNAL ENTRIES FROM OUR AUTHORS*

- *DETAILED AUTHOR BIO'S*

- *CHAPTER EXCERPTS FROM UPCOMING DRY ICE PUBLISHING TITLES*

- *SCHEDULED NEW RELEASE DATES*

MAKE OUR WEB PAGE YOUR HOME PAGE SO YOU DON'T MISS A BEAT!

Send your questions or comments to

info@dryicepublishing.com

Stephen Martini is *the* author of the new millennium! In everything he writes, Martini takes readers from relaxed to riveted.

Martini, who lives and writes in Tennessee, is a former award-winning journalist and author of **Far From Gilded Halls; Finally, Martini Time; The Chattanooga Lookouts & 100 Seasons of Scenic City Baseball;** and the upcoming title, **The Kaleidoscop***e*. He's married to his best friend, Tina, and is "Daddy" to two sons, Zachary and Tyler.

"All men are like grass, and all their glory is like the flowers of the field; the grass withers and the flowers fall, but the word of the Lord stands forever." 1 Peter 1:24-25

Made in United States
North Haven, CT
21 April 2022

18462134R00171